WORK &
REWARDS
IN THE
VIRTUAL
WORKPLACE

WORK & REWARDS IN THE VIRTUAL WORKPLACE

A "New Deal" for Organizations & Employees

N. Fredric Crandall, Ph.D.
Marc J. Wallace, Jr., Ph.D.

AMACOM
American Management Association
New York • Atlanta • Chicago • Kansas City • San Francisco • Washington, D.C.
Brussels • Mexico City • Tokyo • Toronto

Library of Congress Cataloging-in-Publication Data

Crandall, N. Fredric.
    Work & rewards in the virtual workplace : a "new
deal" for organizations & employees / N. Fredric Crandall,
Marc J. Wallace, Jr.
        p.   cm.
    Includes index.
    ISBN 0-8144-0375-1
    1. Human-computer interaction.   2. Virtual reality.
3. Work environment.   I. Wallace, Marc J., 1944-   . II. Title.
QA76.9.H65C73   1998
331.25—dc21   98-17092
                                                                                    CIP

Printing number

10   9   8   7   6   5   4   3   2   1

Tom Mahoney
Thank you for your dedication and mentorship
through our years of training, and thank you for
your watchful eyes in the years since.

Contents

Preface

This book is a guide to workforce effectiveness. It shares the knowledge and experience of front-running organizations that have succeeded in forging technology and people by creating a virtual workplace, and discusses the concept of a New Deal for those who work in it. We will take you through a journey beginning with an overview of powerful economic and social forces shaping the future of work and ending with recommendations for actions that employees and employers alike must take to be successful.

Chapter 1, *Forging a New Compact Between People and Technology*, sets the stage by explaining the new competition, the virtual workplace, and the New Deal.

Chapter 2, *Working the Virtual Workplace*, describes the terminology and concepts of the virtual workplace in detail. We describe how the phenomena of immersion and navigation define the virtual workplace, and we introduce three models of the virtual workplace that cover a broad spectrum of the changes we see taking shape.

Chapter 3, *Exploring the Virtual Workplace*, explores three successive models of the virtual workplace that have developed. We will show how the workplace must adapt to achieve each model and the implications for work and rewards.

Chapter 4, *Work Design*, presents the first major dimension of the virtual workplace. We show how, in the virtual workplace, activities align with core business processes and away from the functional hierarchies that form the basis of traditional organizational work design.

Chapter 5, *Skills and Competencies*, explores the kind of work that will be required in virtual workplaces and how skills and competencies will differ dramatically from those currently deployed in traditional organizations. We provide a commonsense approach to thinking about skills and competencies in a world that often seems committed to making the subject too complex.

Chapter 6, *Rewards in the Virtual Workplace*, examines how the role of rewards and compensation changes when an organization evolves from a traditional to a virtual workplace. Our experience has convinced us that rewards will also be the critical crucible where the New Deal is struck.

Chapter 7, *The Blended Workforce*, describes the increasing prevalence of a virtual employee population comprised of workers directly employed by their company and those who are employed on an assignment or contractual basis, and the importance to business success of correctly managing this mix.

Chapter 8, *The Economics of the Virtual Workplace*, provides a means of assessing the financial feasibility of moving to the virtual workplace. Using easy-to-follow steps, we guide you through the collection of data and the logical arguments to arrive at real figures for making solid decisions.

Chapter 9, *Getting to the New Deal in the Virtual Workplace*, shows the steps you must take to succeed in forging technology and people by creating a virtual workplace, and discusses careers in the New Deal for those who work in it.

Acknowledgments

Curiosity led to the development of this book. It caused us to recognize major shifts in the workplace, such as technological sophistication and workforce displacement, and it forced us to use the tools of research to explore their underlying causes.

We are indebted to many people who encouraged and enabled our curiosity. First, our clients who have shared their experiences with us and allowed us free rein in asking questions and seeking answers: John Riordan and Lea Ann Walters of Sony Electronics; Rug Altmansberger of Corning, Inc.; Maggi Coil of Motorola (now a principal of CWE); Dwain Beidler of Smith & Nephew Orthopaedics; Jean Alden-Lydon of Rich SeaPak; and Michael Snipes and Tom Kovolka of Allstate Insurance. All have provided insights over the years and a realistic test for the ideas in this book.

Several members of CWE have provided invaluable help in the development of the topics included in this book. John Bremen and Mary Shulze contributed to the development of the skill and competency models presented in Chapter 5. Their consulting experience in this area is recognized widely in our field. Marc John Wallace III educated us on the principles behind the economic modeling explored in Chapter 8. We also greatly appreciate the support of Sandy Prestine and Francesca Fell, who have helped us through this endeavor.

A special thanks goes to Dan Cohen, who tirelessly assisted

us in putting our ideas together and structuring them. His in-valuable work helped make this book a reality. He became in-fected with our curiosity and in turn spurred us on.

We also wish to thank Adrienne Hickey, our editor at AMACOM, for disciplining us to get closure on the book.

Finally, we thank our families for their support. Julie Cran-dall and Nancy Wallace have supported our work since we were in graduate school together at the University of Minnesota In-dustrial Relations Center. We are grateful for their understand-ing and encouragement.

WORK & REWARDS IN THE VIRTUAL WORKPLACE

1

Forging a New Compact Between People and Technology

We are living amongst the wreckage and casualties of those who believe the answers to the business problems of today lie in downsizing or replacing people with technology. At the same time we are witnessing the advent of an age of virtual organizations that is creating unprecedented wealth and economic opportunity. Such enterprises can succeed only if they effectively marry people and technology to achieve workforce effectiveness. The place where this is happening is the *virtual workplace*, a work environment that is bound by neither time nor space, where work gets done by people in harmony with technology to create goods and services on demand. There is a seamless interface among people working together in one place at one time, at different places and at different times, or any other combination that successfully meets customer requirements and demands. That is what this book is about.

The New Competition

Economic and technological forces have converged in this last decade of the twentieth century to create an entirely new form of business competition. The *New Competition* encompasses a global economy and is driven by information rather than product and by time rather than space, creating a revolution in the way we do business. At Motorola, for example, designers, engineers, and manufacturing experts are networked in a single production function that reaches from Chicago to Singapore and from Beijing, China, to Frankfurt, Germany. The work takes advantage of the most qualified, available individuals in the world and is occurring somewhere, at any given moment, twenty-four hours a day.

Over the past decade, companies as diverse as Kellogg's, Ford Motor Company, and Coca-Cola have transformed themselves from being U.S.-based companies with operations in other countries to being truly global entities whose core business processes span not only geography but time and space. This process of "going global" has led to vastly different ways of getting work done.

The era of mass customization is upon us. Companies like Gateway 2000 build and ship customized computers in the time it used to take to deliver standard models from inventory. People working in these companies must have broader skills and more diverse competencies than we ever imagined requiring of employees.

The New Competition has created both opportunities and threats and is marked by massive restructuring of businesses on an unparalleled scale. Opportunities have taken the form of untapped markets for global goods and services. Threats have taken the form of unexpected market competition. Corning, Inc., a master of using joint ventures to leverage technology, provides a good example of such opportunities and threats. Its joint venture with Sony Electronics, called American Video Glass, creates opportunity by combining glass technology with unique, high-value markets. At the same time, the New Competition allows a company like Nippon Electric Glass (NEG) to enter Corning's home turf of North America.

Chain Reactions in Conflict

Ultimately, the New Competition has unleashed two parallel chain reactions that have come to be at odds with each other as outlined in Figure 1.1.

Chain reaction 1 is the economic side of the New Competition. Global competition has forced companies to drive down costs in order to remain competitive. The search for efficiency has led to a frenzy of restructuring, reengineering, and downsizing that has touched virtually every major corporation and millions of workers. In the last decade an incredible number of U.S. firms were acquired, merged, and downsized. The job loss, traditionally experienced among blue-collar workers, this time centered on white-collar workers. One study estimates that between 1985 and 1995 almost fourteen million white-collar jobs disappeared.[1]

This first chain of events leads all too often to a strategy of continuous cost reduction and downsizing. It is creating economic dislocation including job loss, career interruption, and

Figure 1.1 Two Chains in Conflict

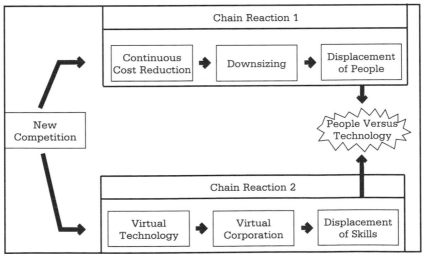

lowered personal income expectations. People in their late forties and fifties are the ones most vulnerable and the ones hardest hit. The *Old Deal*, defining the employment relationship as an implicit contract under which employee loyalty is rewarded with career employment and retirement, has been rudely shattered.

Chain reaction 2 runs parallel to chain reaction 1. It is the technological side of the New Competition and is driven by automation and innovation in information technology. It has changed the relationship between people and machines. Work has transformed from physically manipulating things to managing the flow of paced machines creating products or performing services. We have become a nation of knowledge workers. Information technology has changed the way work is done between physical locations. No longer is it necessary for all people to work at a common site. Now work traverses time and space. New forms of work and organization are forming in cyberspace, making many traditional jobs and skills obsolete. This phenomenon has been named the *virtual organization*.

The result of chain reaction 2 is the displacement of skills. The virtual organization has created tremendous opportunity for work to be done anywhere, by anyone—provided he or she has the requisite skills. Unfortunately, the skills in demand are rarely the skills represented by the population at large.

The two chain reactions have created a terrible conflict between people and technology, raising two important questions:

1. *How will work get done in virtual organizations?* New combinations of people and technology are being shaped into the virtual workplace. The virtual workplace often combines the efforts of people in diverse venues with people from numerous corporate entities working together on a common site, or with former competitors. In each situation, what skills and competencies are needed to assure success? How can effective working relationships and common goals and objectives be engineered among people coming from such different "places"? Today's challenge is to develop an alignment of work design, skills, and

rewards that support a virtual workforce effectiveness, one that can move a business beyond the boundaries of traditional and high-performance organizations to create competitive advantage in this new environment.

   2. *What will the relationship between organizations and employees look like?* The Old Deal—expectations of employees for extended employment—is gone. In order to develop a *New Deal* for employment, how must the work and rewards system supporting a virtual workplace be structured? Once this question is answered, a realistic compact between employer and employee can be developed to make the virtual workplace work.

Will I Be Here Next Year? Do I Want to Be Here Next Year?

Many companies talk as if they have a new approach to employment, but in reality, the majority of our corporations are behaving and reacting according to old habits. They are still downsizing when they should be investing in growth, for example. They are spending millions of dollars to separate one group of people while spending millions more to search for key competencies in other people. They are also sending mixed messages—saying one thing and doing something else.

   In the short term, this kind of duplicity has driven a stake between corporations and their employees. It has created the specter of a land inhabited by the "haves"—corporations, Wall Street, and the investment community, who are enjoying the longest sustained run-up of share values in U.S. history—at the expense of the "have nots"—the shocked, dismayed, and once-loyal employees across North America who feel disenfranchisement and a betrayal of trust. Some "have-nots" left corporate America, taking early out and reduction-in-force retirement packages. Others are jumping from organization to organization. Still others have found themselves without employment or employability. The result is a tremendous sense of cynicism and bitterness.

At the same time, continuous downsizing destroys a company's future. The habit destroys a firm's ability to acquire and deploy the very competencies it will need in the long run to compete with better staffed virtual organizations. In fact, we have achieved a level of employee disenfranchisement (especially among white-collar workers) that has provided the AFL-CIO the greatest opportunity for growth in membership seen since the 1930s. This malaise is best summed up by one manager who, having survived three major downsizings in as many years, said, "I've gone from wondering if I'll be here next year, to wondering, 'Why would I want to be here next year?'"

The New Competition and Virtual Organizations

The New Competition has emerged in three parallel developments:

1. Former competitors forming alliances to command the market
2. New marriages of technology, markets, and opportunity
3. The creation of new business entities that replace traditional ones, defining the entire length of a value chain— a form of organization that has been characterized as the virtual organization

Alliances of Former Competitors

The first manifestation of the New Competition is the prospect of former competitors joining forces to create new markets or protect current intellectual property. An example of this is Sematech, the joint venture formed by Intel (supplying the technology behind IBM's personal computers) and Motorola (supplying the technology behind Apple's computers) to create future generations of technology. Similarly, Dow Chemical and E.I. DuPont have joint-ventured new chemical processes.

New Marriages—Strategic Alliances

At a more sophisticated level, the New Competition has generated marriages of technology, markets, and opportunity. Microsoft and NBC, for example, have created MSNBC, a venture that will create an entirely new market combining the worlds of information, entertainment, and communication. Similarly, Disney is joint-venturing with software developers and toy makers to redefine the leisure market.

Virtual Organizations

Ultimately, we are witnessing the emergence of an entirely new form of organization called the *virtual organization*, the seamless integration of numerous elements of the value chain. Virtual organizations can take many forms and include both temporary and permanent relationships. Key elements are an integration that is customer-focused and utilization of a combination of technology and people to obtain extraordinary competitive advantage. Many examples already exist:

- Borg-Warner is managing Ford's transmission inventories, providing product on demand in a seamless, instantaneous process that requires almost no standing inventory in Ford assembly plants.
- West Bend provides Wal-Mart with 100 percent fill rates on all product lines by linking Wal-Mart's point of sale information system directly with West Bend's manufacturing operation.

What do we know about these developments and how they affect business processes? Joint ventures, strategic alliances, and virtual organizations are increasing rapidly, by some estimates as much as 25 percent per year. Although the research output is not large yet, two facts have come to light:

1. *Speed of execution, being ahead of your competition, is critical.*
Experts point out that the first player creating a new market
commands perhaps 80 percent of that market by the time the second and third players enter. The result creates tremendous barriers to entry, favoring those who get there first.[2]

2. *Getting into a virtual arrangement is not without risk.* A successful alliance is one that lasts five to ten years. Experts estimate
the success rate (so defined) to be about 50 to 60 percent.[3]

Breaking the rules on traditional competitive relationships
among companies has helped give rise to the virtual corporation. Strategic and innovative utilization of technology and people has also been instrumental in the development of how work
is done in the virtual corporation. But any time the nature of a
corporation changes so radically, the structure of the organization, how people do work, and how they are rewarded, must
also change quickly and efficiently in order to attain competitive
advantage in the marketplace.

The virtual organization requires a virtual workplace. The
virtual workplace is a work environment where goods and services are created and delivered joining employees beyond the
traditional bounds of time and place. Technology is a foundation
for the virtual workplace, creating the means for innovations in
working relationships such as teams of people who work together via teleconferencing or transfer work in progress from
one venue to the next across time zones to keep work going on a
continuous basis. We will explore the way virtual work is done
in greater depth in Chapter 2.

The Demise of the Old Deal for Work and Rewards

Amidst the massive restructuring and the move to virtual
arrangements, a void has emerged. The social contract, or Old
Deal, between employer and employee has disintegrated. The

devastating personal, financial, and emotional toll has been poignantly documented by many analysts. It has been graphically depicted as a vast restructuring that has overtaken corporate America with a devastating toll in job loss, disrupted careers, and threatened families. We have in effect thrown out the traditional work compact; we have abruptly changed how we work, our earnings, and our economic security. *We believe that the demise of the old deal is the single most important factor that will challenge our economy in the next decade.* However, we have not yet filled this void with an acceptable, effective social contract we can call the New Deal. While some companies are beginning to take steps in this direction, most are not yet directly facing the challenges of the social and economic realities requiring a New Deal. For example, the following is definitely *not* the New Deal:

1. *Cost-cutting–focused restructuring.* Unfortunately, the promise of a dramatic reinvention of business through process redesign (or restructuring, reengineering, or any other term) has not achieved the high expectations initially set. The job loss associated with the process rarely coincides with truly more powerful work designs. Nor have clear messages been transmitted to those remaining about the nature of employment opportunities in the future. With the massive layoffs, lack of truly powerful change, and without a clear message having been sent to employees, this form of restructuring leaves more questions about the future than it answers. Management expert Dan Tapscott and strategy experts Hamel and Prahalad claim that this incomplete form of restructuring is a dead end because in practice it focuses only on getting costs down, not creating value.[4]

2. *Downsizing.* Like anorexia nervosa, downsizing has become a life-threatening pattern among companies who seem to utilize it as the management strategy of the 1990s. The victim sheds weight well past the point of balanced health with the result that healthy tissue is lost, sickness sets in, and ultimately the victim dies.

This type of corporate restructuring does not promote an effective new deal message. Consider the conflicting message sent by downsizing: "Sorry, but it's a jungle out there. We've got to save the ship, even if it means that we drop you at will. For those of you remaining, we expect you to do more with less, be empowered to take risks, and devote your energies and attention to making us successful!" The results are, predictably, a survivor's syndrome of guilt, fear, cynicism, and depression.

3. *Proclaiming.* Several leading companies facing the economic contingencies of restructuring and reengineering have crafted and proclaimed "New Deal statements" that read like mission statements. These statements are typically not backed up by substantive measures that create a new employment compact. Their logic reads something like this:

> There are no employment guarantees anymore. Ultimately, employment security lies with our customers. The company's job is to do our best in creating markets, being first with new technology and process, and providing opportunities for growth. The employees' obligation is to manage themselves as assets. Their major opportunity for continuing employment is to continue to add value to the business.

Leaving employees on their own to persevere does not really do much good. Saying it over and over again doesn't make it happen. Employees may listen at first, and persevere, but ultimately the message is hollow and cynicism sets in. Predictably, survey research shows us that employee commitment to organizations has dropped severely over recent years to an all-time low.[5]

These trends have shocked and dismayed once-loyal employees across North America. Some have opted out, while others jump from company to company, only to see themselves immersed in the same game at a different venue. The sense of frustration and the mixed messages sent by employers who are simultaneously laying people off while desperately trying to hire those with needed skills is clear evidence that a truly *New* Deal has not yet fully emerged.

The New Deal Defined: The Components of Workforce Effectiveness

Just what is this New Deal? What does it look like? And how do we get there? The New Deal for work and rewards is taking shape at this moment. Those companies that are forging this New Deal have found that it differs from a traditional, implicit employment contract with regard to skills, work design, and rewards (including compensation, employment, and tenure with the organization), as outlined in Figure 1.2.

Figure 1.2 Comparison of the Old Deal and the New Deal

	Old Deal	*New Deal*
Skills	• Hold skills constant and vary head count	• Hold head count constant and grow skills
Work Design	• Define work by jobs and functions	• Define work by business process
	• Define compensation by a job's estimated labor market value	• Define compensation by the value the work adds to the business process
Rewards Employment, and Tenure	• Everyone is an employee and has a job for life	• There exists a blended workforce comprised of core, support, and temporary employees retained as long as the business need continues

Skills

Under the Old Deal, technology and markets were relatively static and insulated. A company established its processes, hired mostly semi-skilled and unskilled workers, and managed production by varying head count. (For example, this approach is often used in traditional automobile manufacturing.) Skills were held constant and managers adjusted to swings in demand through layoffs and hiring.

Under the New Deal, technology is rapidly and constantly changing. Physical work has transitioned to knowledge work. Successful competitors have learned to hold head count constant—even in the face of fluctuating demand—by (1) running "lean" with a core workforce; (2) enhancing, growing, and renewing the skills resident among core employees; and (3) facilitating access to additional skills when needed on an assignment or temporary basis. (We will discuss this in detail in our treatment of the blended workforce in Chapter 7.) When companies invest heavily in skill acquisition among their core employees, they protect both the employee and the corporation over changes in the business cycle.

Work Design

In a traditional organization, work is compartmentalized into narrow jobs or positions, defined by functional and occupational domains. The result is disjointed execution, high unit cost, and uncompetitively long cycle times.

In the New Deal there are no narrow jobs. Departments and functional domains have disappeared. Work is bundled into fluid teams. The members of these teams have a far greater depth and breadth of skills than they would have in traditional jobs. In addition, the teams often include employees from more than one company. This versatility in work design allows an employee to take an entire business process from start to finish in one rapid, seamless flow. In the Old Deal there might have been one hundred separate job classifications in a facility. In the New

Deal, the same facility might run with ten or fewer broadly defined roles.

Rewards

In the Old Deal, a person's pay level was dictated by the estimated labor market value of the job held. Under the New Deal, jobs have gone away, and so has much of the relevance of internal job evaluation and the whole kit of traditional compensation tools. In addition, automatic annual raises and pay hierarchies have became a thing of the past.

In the New Deal, total compensation is driven primarily by the economic impact of employees' skills on core business processes. The more impact one has on critical processes and the more one can do to increase speed and improve productivity, quality, and financial results, the more money one will make, primarily through variable pay.

Employment and Tenure

Under the Old Deal, everyone was a "permanent" regular employee. The utilization of temporary employees was the exception. The New Deal, however, is characterized by a *blended workforce*—one comprised of core, support, and temporary employees.

Human asset investment (skill acquisition and training) shifts from being exclusively the responsibility of the company to one that is shared with employees. The company is responsible for growing and maintaining "core" competencies while employees are responsible for developing, maintaining, and renewing their basic skills.

Under the Old Deal, a job became an implicit sinecure. The job emerged during the post-World War II era as an asset to which an employee gained implicit title through loyalty and longevity. In the New Deal, there are no lifetime guarantees. The most a company can realistically assure is employment as long as the business need continues. Events require both employer and employee to behave more like entrepreneurs, because employment opportunity is created only through business success. However, the New Deal must be clear on the value companies invest in human capital. For "core" employees, greater longevity will be the natural outcome of developing a broad range of skills that are of particular value to the company. Companies will be more likely to make long-term commitments in people who have obtained more "core" skills than those with fewer ancillary skills.

If America is to thrive in the economy of the twenty-first century, it must not allow the current competition between people and technology to continue—the fight between John Henry and the steam engine. Rather, we must marry the two chain reactions. We must integrate people and technology in ways that allow all stakeholders (companies, employees, shareholders, and customers) to thrive in the next century.

Integrating the technological and economic tracks will require us to shift our paradigms from one of "people *versus* technology" to one of "people *plus* technology." The latter is truly a workforce effectiveness model that carries the key to competitive advantage. It's quite simple. Those companies that achieve workforce effectiveness will win. Those that don't will lose.

Why Go Virtual? An Issue of Competitive Advantage

If you are still asking "Why go virtual?" here are some reasons to look beyond your current world.

Before America was discovered, the question of whether the earth was round or flat was simply idle conversation. Once the new land was discovered, however, the shape of the earth became important because it became *an issue of competitive advantage.* If we could be certain we wouldn't fall off the other side of the earth, we could go in search of new frontiers. Indeed, with the knowledge that the earth was round—and that there were lands beyond the one on which we stood—new opportunities and worlds opened up to us.

The virtual revolution offers a similar competitive advantage, but, like the shape of the earth, not everyone immediately perceives or accepts virtual reality. The competitive advantage afforded by virtual reality and the virtual workplace become apparent only when you can see your industry and your competitors experimenting with virtual concepts and constructs. It's then that the immersive systems become real and the virtual workplace becomes an issue of survival, not just coffee table chit-chat.

Before long, going virtual will be the only way to achieve process and quality improvements of any magnitude. Today's virtual companies do things in hours instead of days and for pennies instead of dollars. Their quality improvements measure six *times* better, not six *percent* better. Asking, "Why go virtual?" today is like Henry Ford asking many years ago, "Why switch to the assembly line to manufacture automobiles?" If you don't go virtual, you'll soon be out of business. The information age has made virtual technology and concepts imperative. If you want to ride the crest and survive the information age, you're going to have to jump in.

Notes

1. L. Uchitelle and N. R. Kleinfeld, "On the Battlefields of Business, Millions of Casualties," *New York Times*, March 3, 1996, 1.

2. Gary Hamel and C.K. Prahalad, *Competing for the Future*. Boston: Harvard Business School Press, 1994.

3. Damian McNamara, "The Alliance Edge," *Chemical Marketing Reporter*, July 24, 1995, SR11.

4. Don Tapscott, *The Digital Economy*. New York: McGraw-Hill, 1996, 183; and Hamel & Prahalad, 205.

5. Brian O'Reilly, "The New Deal," *Fortune*, June 13, 1994, 44.

2

Working in the Virtual Workplace

The virtual revolution is transforming the business world. It is characterized by electronic information technology, new work arrangements, incredible speed, and a pervasive service mentality. It is the most significant event businesses have experienced since the Industrial Revolution.

The electronic technology that has unleashed the virtual revolution—e-mail systems, modems, cellular phones, teleconferencing centers, laptops, and more—is spurring significant changes in workplace systems and design. Businesses on the leading edge of the revolution are changing *everything*. They're overhauling work systems, upgrading and broadening employees' skill bases, and revamping reward systems to maximize their use of technology and enhance workforce effectiveness. They're combining emerging technologies with creative employment arrangements, contingency-based pay, customer/supplier partnerships, and more to enable employees to work from anywhere at any time. These companies have the motive, opportunity, and processes they need to move ahead of the competition, producing lower-priced, higher-quality products and services faster and more efficiently than ever before. Their motive is survival and the desire to thrive, to leave the competition in the dust in a competitive worldwide economy.

Technology provides businesses with the opportunity to speed products and services to the customer on request, and the virtual workplace provides the framework for the process. A good example of this is a story told by one of the U.S.-based managers interviewed for this book. His company had the opportunity, along with five or six competitors, to bid on work for a Western European client. With experts assembled all over the world, this manager's company was instantly able to assemble a team to put together a project bid and personally sell it to the client before its competitors had even begun to consider *their* approach to the work. The customer was so impressed with the company's speed in putting together a clean, intelligent project bid that it awarded the company the project without hesitation. Today, the manager's company does 85 percent of the contract work for that Western European company.

As this example demonstrates, employees in the virtual workplace are customer-focused. Everyone in the organization is capable of selling its products and services, and employees work from anywhere and everywhere to meet and exceed customer expectations.

In this chapter we will define the vocabulary of this new world and discuss what makes the virtual workplace different from traditional places of work. We will also consider three models of virtual workplaces that describe the continuum of options and answer the question, "How virtual is it?" Finally, we will examine how workforce effectiveness and its components of work design, skills, and rewards change as an organization goes virtual.

Defining Terms

While the terms *virtual reality, virtual corporation,* and *virtual product* have appeared in the popular press, it can be difficult to understand exactly what they mean. The following definitions will facilitate our discussion of work and rewards in the virtual organization.

Virtual Workplace

The virtual workplace is defined by the "anytime, anywhere" qualities we've come to associate with virtual reality. When we talk about a virtual workplace (VWP), we're describing networks of people—not bound by the traditional limitations of time, physical space, one hundred-word job descriptions, titles, pyramidal reporting relationships, and the like—who are engaged in work. This workplace is far from static; the only constant thing about it is its customer orientation. Otherwise, it changes moment by moment, based on the needs of customers, suppliers, employees, and producers.

The virtual workplace isn't bound by visual or physical proximity. It's literally anywhere work is done: an airplane, a bed-and-breakfast in Europe, an employee's home. The virtual workplace exists as a platform to conceive, produce, and deliver a virtual product or service.

Virtual Reality

Virtual reality (VR) can be defined as time, space, and substance that exist in effect but not in fact. For example, a flight simulator running on a personal computer provides the experience of flying a plane from the comfort of a desk. The desk and computer become a virtual cockpit. Virtual reality involves creating and transporting images and information through time and space to create the experience of "being there."

VR technology includes elements such as audio and video transmission; head-mounted displays; devices that guide computerized instructions, such as keyboards, pointing devices, or gloves; and electronic computerized systems that drive the devices. As shown in Figure 2.1, the effectiveness of VR can be tracked along two dimensions or axes:[1]

1. *Immersion* is the quality of being "inside" a virtual system. It constitutes the degree to which the virtual experience—in this case, the workplace—is perceived as real, both to insiders (employees) and outsiders (customers).

2. *Navigation* is the ease with which individuals and teams deliberately move around and complete tasks within the virtual workplace. Navigational tools in the virtual workplace include the combination of technology with work and reward systems that help produce the virtual product or service. For example, the Friday meetings you hold with your sales reps in a virtual "conference room" with online teleconferencing might be one navigational tool your organization uses. It is the unique combination of people's work roles, skills, and reward systems—*all tied to technology*—that makes the virtual workplace work.

The question of "How virtual is it?" is answered as a function of immersion and navigation. For example, a computer running DOS allows the same outcomes as one that has implemented a desktop metaphor such as Windows. Both interfaces allow for the retrieval of files, but the desktop metaphor facili-

Figure 2.1   Tracking Virtual Reality Along Two Axes

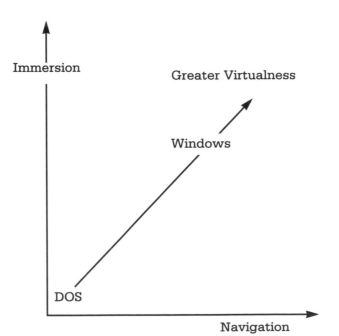

tates the experience of retrieving information in the same way one would retrieve it in an office: by locating documents on a desktop or storing them in a file folder. Thus, the desktop metaphor represents a superior level of immersion. Similarly, using a "find" command to locate a file is a navigational strategy that is better than looking through endless subdirectories. In effect, VR provides the opportunity to structure problems and their solutions in a digitally driven, real-time analog to reality. VR technology is being used widely to solve mathematical and scientific problems, and its use in training simulations for aerospace and defense is well-known, as is its application in recreation and entertainment. Although still in the rudimentary stages of development and application, VR principles have begun, but only barely begun, to reshape business organizations and the work performed in them.

The Virtual Corporation, Virtual Product, and Virtual Service

VR has resulted in the evolution of virtual corporations and virtual products. Organizations are discovering that virtual technologies can provide the means to get people together to share information, complete tasks, and greatly speed up product delivery.

The virtual corporation typically will fit the following description:

> To the outside observer [the virtual corporation] will appear almost edgeless, with permeable and continuously changing interfaces between company, supplier, and customer. From inside the firm the view will be no less amorphous, with traditional offices, departments, and operating divisions constantly reforming according to need. Job responsibilities will regularly shift, as will lines of authority—even the very definition of *employee* will change, as some customers and suppliers

begin to spend more time in the company than will some of the firm's own workers.[2]

The virtual product or virtual service is defined by its instantaneous availability at any time, in any place, and in any variety. The capability to produce the product or service at any time, in any place, and in any variety is defined as its "virtualness." While the product definition/description exists in virtual reality, its real analog is produced instantaneously by people in the VR organization. The evolution of VR technology has created the *possibility* of virtual products; the evolution of the virtual organization has created the capacity to *deliver* the virtual product.

In many respects, virtual products are the hyperextension of the just-in-time revolution of the 1980s.[3] During this revolution, traditional bureaucratic organizations were transformed by customer-driven demands to deliver products and services of higher quality in reduced time frames. This led many organizations to restructure or re-engineer around critical work processes to deliver specific products or services to individual customers at specific levels of quality at specific times.

The virtual product is produced by a cooperative network that includes combinations of suppliers, manufacturers, and customers. The virtual product can be delivered almost instantaneously because product specifications, production capability, and delivery are online, and can be made available to all network participants simultaneously. Roles in the process are defined at the moment the product is conceived, and which individuals represent each organization may not be clear to outsiders. Relationships change and reshape for each successive product or service. Virtual products have been around for many years. American Airlines revolutionized the airline ticket by initiating the SABRE System in the early 1960s and has continued to revolutionize its virtual product (see sidebar 2.1).

How a virtual organization produces a virtual product is exemplified by the role of engineer John Chabot, who works for Ross Operating Valve Co. of Troy, Michigan. Chabot's work in-

---

2.1   An Early Virtual Product

The concept of virtual products is not all that new. AMR, the parent company of American Airlines, Inc., initiated the SABRE system in the early 1960s, which initially allowed travel agents to access a computerized network and design a highly customized product—i.e., an airline ticket and travel itinerary. Eventually, this service was expanded to anyone with a modem. Today, most business travelers cannot imagine life before SABRE. Results of this virtual system include:

■ Significant payroll savings for the airline and the purchaser's agent

■ Almost complete elimination of processing time

■ Capability to offer the product to many more customers

(William H. Davidow and Michael S. Malone, *The Virtual Corporation*. New York: HarperCollins, 1992.)

---

volves networking with suppliers and customers, engineering products, and working with databases as well as producing the actual valves. According to one description of Chabot's role:

> Not only does Chabot design valves . . . he also sells them to customers and works closely with the machinery and testing operations. He and his coworkers assist customers in designing their own valves for their particular needs. Then Ross produces and delivers them as fast as possible, sometimes in as little as 24 hours.[4]

Chabot describes his role in the following way: "I design it, I machine it, test it [sic], make sure it's ready to ship to the customer. And when the customer gets it, I interact with him to make improvements or change design. We're really more of a process than a product."

Though the virtual revolution is fairly young, many organizations have been experimenting with virtual workplace approaches. An example of one such experiment is TBWA Chiat/Day, an advertising firm in New York City. In 1994, almost all of the firm's 158 employees created their own schedules on a day-to-day basis, coming in to the office or staying home, working from a client's location, or from a house on the beach. The firm didn't require employees to work a 40-hour week just to satisfy their clients. What employees were asked to remember as they planned their days, however, was that work arrangements were task-driven, set up by individuals and work teams that kept client and coworker needs in mind at all times (see sidebar 2.2).

2.2   TBWA Chiat/Day and the Virtual Office

TBWA Chiat/Day, an advertising agency, has eliminated offices and instead has created areas that are designed to accomplish a specific task. Employees are given a cellular phone and laptop computer, and they go wherever necessary to accomplish a task. Chiat/Day's major technological wizardry in this effort lies in its phone system, which is able to route incoming calls immediately to employees wherever they may be, as if they were in traditional offices down the hall. As a result, employees can work where they feel most productive. More time is spent with clients, in teams working on a campaign in one of the conference rooms, on the road, or even at home. At the same time, Chiat/Day has reduced office and office-related expenses substantially.

(Cleveland Horton, "A Day in the 'Virtual' Life of a Chiat/Day Executive," *Advertising Age*. March 14, 1994, 19–20.)

Organizations experimenting with virtual concepts admit that "going virtual" isn't an easy transition to make. It calls for changes in corporate culture and organizational structure and, as Bob Seibold of Perot Systems Corporation points out, it demands that companies eliminate "'70s leadership in the '90s environment."

Going virtual is a change that's well worth the effort, though. By transforming to the virtual workplace, organizations become able to develop and produce products more quickly; serve their customers better; improve product quality; lower costs, both internally and to the customer; help keep the Earth cleaner; create barriers to entry for competitors that aren't up to speed; and employ happier, healthier people—and that's just the beginning.

Traditional vs. Virtual Workplaces

The virtual workplace isn't bound by time or space. It exists as a platform to conceive, produce, and deliver the virtual product or service. It may involve individual contributors and teams from a number of firms. How does an employee work out of a mobile office? What skills are required to produce the virtual product? How does a virtual team operate? There are no long-established models or road maps to help answer these questions, but many companies are quickly making up their own rules.

The difference between traditional and virtual workplaces is illustrated by the way people talk about their work (see Figure 2.2). A traditional worker says, "I go to work" and "I finish my work." Implied in these statements is the presumption that "work doesn't start until I get there and it stops when I go home."

Thinking of work as if it were attached to time and space limits productivity. For example, one of the greatest problems with "shift work" in manufacturing is the difficulty of capturing and transferring experience and expertise gained on one shift to

Figure 2.2 Defining Work in the Conventional Workplace

"What I do"	*Meaning*
"I go to work."	• Work is centered around me. • I am transported to a physical place where work exists. • What I do is bounded by what I see and where I am.
"I finish my work."	• Work is done when I leave the place where it is done.

the next. Companies have attempted to deal with this problem by creating intershift "bridges" such as logs, notes on bulletin boards, periodic meetings, and, recently, communication via electronic mail systems.

Intel Corp., a leading manufacturer of microprocessor chips, recognized a virtual-workplace opportunity with the ramp-up stage for the manufacturing of a new generation of microprocessors. At this stage, speed is crucial for recapturing investment in technology, a significant competitive advantage. Intel's solution involves "improvement teams," members of work teams from each shift who meet frequently to coordinate their activities, discuss problems, and share solutions.[5] The teams also communicate via electronic mail to accelerate continuous improvement between meetings so that no one has to wait for the next meeting to move forward. Their key to process improvement is using electronic mail to coordinate intershift process improvements and act immediately.

Because work is independent of time and space in the virtual workplace, it is expressed differently (see Figure 2.3). There is a shift in emphasis from "I" to "we" as well as a change in focus toward a process-oriented, continuous work flow. In the virtual workplace, work is driven by the production requirements of the virtual product. The process is repetitive, but the

Figure 2.3 Defining Work in the Virtual Workplace

"What I do"	*Meaning*
"I join in the ongoing work process."	• Work is centered around a process. • The process is ongoing. • There is no beginning or end to the work. • Work can take place anywhere.

product differs to some degree with each instance. Work is not centered on "me," and "I" don't control it by "my" presence. The boundaries of the workplace are determined by the participants, and these limits tend to be broader than the firm or company, extending to include vendors and customers.

The Virtual Workplace

The virtual workplace has been created by moving away from the traditional common-site, common-time workplace through successive levels of immersion and navigation. As companies have experimented with and explored the virtual workplace, we have identified three distinct approaches: the telecommuting, frontline, and cyberlink workplaces.

The *telecommuting* workplace is the entry-level virtual workplace where individual employees work at a distance from their physical place of work and are linked back to it electronically. The *frontline* workplace actually places employees of one company on site with another company as vendor, salesperson or service representative. The *cyberlink* workplace is a workplace integrating elements of a work process that may combine people and resources from many companies. Examples of the cyberlink workplace include integrating a supply chain to create and produce products collaboratively or project management, including numerous contributors and subcontractors, combining resources to complete work for a customer.

Because the virtual workplace is based on the combination of immersion and navigation, these three approaches differ regarding their attributes (see Figure 2.4). Telecommuting represents an advance in navigation through the use of various types of electronic equipment to tie the employee back to the physical workplace. Alternatively, the frontline workplace immerses the representatives of one company into the milieu of another. The cyberlink workplace combines both immersion and navigation into a highly advanced form of work organization. It is not necessary for a company to move step by step through telecommuting and frontline workplaces to get to the cyberlink workplace. However, many companies prefer to take such a step-by-step approach to facilitate the transition.

The Telecommuting Workplace

At GTE Corporation in Stamford, Connecticut, most U.S.-based employees can work from home one to three days a week if their supervisor gives his or her approval. The telecommunications company offers corporate-wide guidelines for telecommuting, but it gives divisions and departments a lot of leeway in establishing their own programs. This kind of flexibility is key, says Francine Riley, retired director of workforce diversity and an eight-year manager of telecommuters, since some divisions and departments are highly technology-dependent and require telecommuters to have access to computers and others aren't but can offer telecommuters an opportunity to take the normal "paperwork" of their job home to complete in a relatively uninterrupted environment. Though there are many advantages to telecommuting, says Riley, one that sums it all up is this: "Telecommuting is one of the few things I've seen that marries [a company's] human resource needs with growing technologies and the needs of our environment."

The telecommuting workplace represents an entry into the virtual workplace from an employee's perspective. Individuals are provided the opportunity, on a voluntary or mandatory basis, to work outside of the office, from their homes or other re-

Figure 2.4 Three Types of Virtual Workplaces

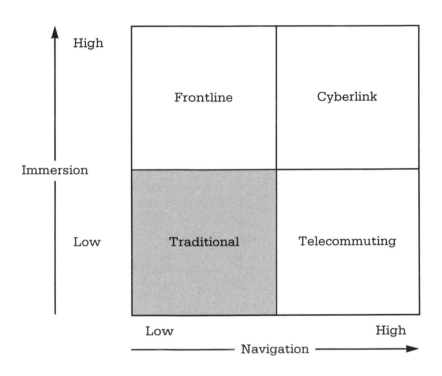

mote locations. Employees communicate with their companies using advanced communications technology, including computers, modems, fax machines, and e-mail. Figure 2.5 summarizes the productivity improvement opportunities and key elements of the telecommuting workplace.

Challenges organizations may encounter while implementing this model have mainly to do with communication and trust between managers and employees. Managers need training in supervising and coaching off-site workers, and employees need time management and technology training. Communication methods also need to be refined to ensure that employees have the organizational support they need to serve the customer. The work systems elements within this model—like traditional benefits, pay, and appraisal processes—can stay basically the same.

Figure 2.5 The Telecommuting Workplace

Productivity Improvement Opportunities: Productivity can be increased through time savings from reduced commuting, balanced against remote communication and interconnection requirements.

Key Elements

1. Work role of employee	Conducts work at a remote site (work that is normally done on site)
2. Role of manager	Requires a nontraditional and flexible style of reporting and feedback
3. Special skills	Is capable of working independently; is a self-starter; manages time well
4. Special requirements	Needs "checkpoint" meetings to maintain social contact with the common site

---

The Frontline Workplace

In Harold "Bud" Boughton's CBS division of Fiserv, a provider of information technology systems, products, and services to the financial community, sales employees operate as if they were running their own businesses. They spend their time working on the road and at customers' sites, carrying a laptop computer complete with word processing and presentation development software. They also have fax machines and cellular phones. "Our customers don't know our salespeople are working in a virtual office," says Boughton, who oversees the virtual sales operation. "On their business cards, our salespeople have the phone number of the sales center they represent. They also have a 24-hour voice mail system that they check every two to three hours during the day and on weekends, and they respond accordingly." Fiserv benefits from this arrangement because it has more productive sales employees who are much more visible to the customer. "The salesperson is also more selective about where he or she spends time," adds Boughton; "they make better choices about where to spend time because they own the business, so they qualify prospects better."

Within the frontline workplace (Figure 2.6), sales and service employees move out of the office individually and in teams to work from remote locations, mobile offices, satellite centers, and customer locations. This workplace blends virtual workplace characteristics—like customer orientation and partnering, and the use of expert systems and telecommunications equipment—with the existing sales culture. Ties to the physical office are loosened and relationships with the customer are strengthened.

Implementing this workplace is more challenging than implementing the telecommuting workplace. Organizations need to define clearly who does what, where, when, and how; get employees out of the office and closer to the customer on a permanent basis; and encourage employees and managers alike to recognize the customer as their boss. Employees may need to be sold on the flexibility and autonomy they'll gain "working from anywhere," and they may need training in the technology that will enable them to do their jobs. Other employee training opportunities exist in customer service, basic office administration, and partnering with customers. Managers may also need to be sold. It's normal for managers to be apprehensive about supervising employees they can't see—particularly when they're still accountable for the results of off-site teams. Nonetheless, they need to trust employees and learn to coach them rather than control them. Fiserv's Boughton has found that trust is generally rewarded. Results Fiserv has seen since implementing its off-site sales program include increased productivity, reduced cost of sales, and increased customer satisfaction.

Figure 2.6 The Frontline Workplace

Productivity Improvement Opportunities: Increased customer face time helps to provide timely resolution of problems and extraordinary customer service.

Key Elements

1. Work role of employee	High degree of focus on customer; minimal contact with other company employees
2. Role of manager	Requires nontraditional and flexible style of reporting and feedback
3. Special skills	Use of technology and expert systems integrated with sales and service role
4. Special requirements	Merging of sales and service capabilities

The Cyberlink Workplace

At VeriFone, a global provider of secure electronic payment solutions for financial institutions, merchants, and consumers, the senior management team and other employees are scattered around the globe. For example, the senior vice president of operations is based in Los Angeles, the vice president of development is in Dallas, and the vice president of sales is based in Atlanta. Is this good for the customer? You bet. Observes William Pape, chief information officer and senior vice president with the company, VeriFone's employees give clients the benefit of 24-hour customer service.

Consider this: A VeriFone employee concluded a meeting with a client in Washington, D.C., at 4:30 P.M. Eastern Standard Time. The employee was eager to incorporate the client's information and feedback into his presentation, so he shared it electronically with company executives in Santa Fe, New Mexico, and Hong Kong. The VeriFone employees collaborated on the presentation overnight so that by 8:30 the next morning Washington time, the first VeriFoner was able to return to the client with information that had been tailored to the client's needs. Notes Pape:

> "When the customer walked out the door at 4:30 last night, he shut down. Nothing happened in his company. So to have someone walk in the next morning who has obviously done a huge amount of thinking on the subject since you last left him looks like magic to people. This way, we get to work a problem twenty-four hours a day, and clients get the synergy of three or four people all working on the same problem, which can be tremendously powerful."

The cyberlink workplace (Figure 2.7) represents the greatest level of 'virtualness' an organization so far has achieved. Within this workplace, work is managed collaboratively, integrating the whole value chain from the production of goods and services right through to the customer. Teams of employees and customers work together in a flexible, virtual environment that transcends traditional time and geographical boundaries. They remain virtually linked, exchanging ideas and information in person and electronically—*and sometimes never even meeting face to face*—until business opportunities have been fully realized. By broadening the virtual workplace to include customers and suppliers, you make your organization vulnerable; but you also open the door to teams of people who can enhance and improve your products and services, bringing to the table fresh ideas and new ways of doing things.

The most challenging step of all is the reconstruction of work systems around virtual reality. It's here that reward systems are revamped, performance management systems opened up to include customers and suppliers, work roles arranged and

Figure 2.7 The Cyberlink Workplace

Productivity Improvement Opportunities: Achieve dramatic process improvements as measured in terms of time, service, cost, quality, and revenue.

Key Elements

1. Work role of employee	Works with others using a diverse skill set to deliver products and services unique to each customer
2. Role of manager	Transition to coach and coordinator
3. Special skills	Capability to work on teams with expert systems and advanced communications equipment
4. Special requirements	Technological and social networks

rearranged, teams formed and disbanded; the work environment appears to have few structures holding it in place. What seems from the outside like chaos, however, is actually flexibility: day-to-day, customer-dependent change that the virtual workplace requires and thrives on. It's this flexibility that enables cyberlink workplaces to produce high-quality products and services practically on demand.

Organizations that choose to go virtual don't have to step through the workplaces outlined above. Some may launch their virtual work environment with the frontline workplace; others may decide to jump into a cyberlink workplace, partnering with customers and suppliers as a first step. The most successful virtual workplaces will blend state-of-the-art information technology with a restructured, flexible organizational design and proven workforce effectiveness tools. Making the transformation work will require open minds, creative problem-solving skills, and innovative human resource management.

Workforce Effectiveness in the Virtual Workplace

Workforce effectiveness has three major components, whether in traditional, high-performance, or virtual organizations: work design, skills and competencies, and rewards. These components drive performance and execute strategic objectives. Effective work systems require alignment of all three components.

The evolution from traditional to high-performance organizations ratcheted work roles from an individual focus to a team focus. In addition, employees acquired broader skill bases, breaking down boundaries between nonexempt and exempt work and white-collar and blue-collar work. Rewards systems were transformed, and broad-based incentives and competency-based pay programs were developed to support the execution of high-performance work systems. In high-performance organizations, workforce effectiveness enabled companies to achieve competitive advantage through increased flexibility and speed, and it enabled a transition to a process-flow framework. Figure 2.8 demonstrates how the three components of workforce effectiveness impact the execution of strategy.

The challenge of workforce effectiveness in the virtual organization is to move beyond the boundaries of the traditional and high-performance organization to create competitive advantage in this new environment. In order to illustrate this point, consider how different the purchase of a homeowners' insurance policy twenty years ago is from the way it is done today. Twenty years ago one contacted an agent who made a date to visit three days later. The agent carried many pounds of binders, papers, and brochures to the meeting. He wrote down lengthy details concerning specifics on a multi-page application. Many questions had to be answered with responses such as "I really can't say—let me check with the home office and get back to you." There was little choice in coverages; only basic types of policies were available. The application was submitted by mail and put

Figure 2.8 How Workforce Effectiveness Drives
Execution of Strategy

Work Design +	Skills +	Rewards =	Execution
What people are asked to do and how activities are organized	Competencies and skills needed to obtain results	Messages sent, behavior rewarded, career opportunities offered	• Speed • Flexibility • Profitability • Process improve-ment • Customer responsive-ness

into a batch-processing room, where it sat for two days before beginning a long, disjointed approval process.

Over the years, the traditional insurance application process has given way to a high-performance structure with fewer players and handoffs. As Figure 2.9 shows, a team replaces individual contributors, and productivity is improved by streamlining the process and introducing versatility of roles to the team. Cycle time and cost have been reduced.

What does this process look like in a virtual organization? A virtual insurance application radically changes the way products are conceived, developed, and delivered. The agent works with a laptop computer on the client's premises to assess needs, create the policy, and issue it on the spot. The cost is reduced greatly, and cycle time to policy issue is almost instantaneous. Instead of a work team at the home office, the agent works with an expert system residing in the computer as well as with expert specialists in the home office who aid with online advice, if and when needed. This process is coming to be known as *mass customization*. Figure 2.9 shows how the process has been streamlined.

In this example, deliberate changes to work design, skills, and rewards were required to support the evolution of insurance sales. Work design moves almost completely outside of the "home office" to the laptop computer with its expert systems in

Figure 2.9 Traditional vs. High-Performance vs. Virtual Insurance Application Process

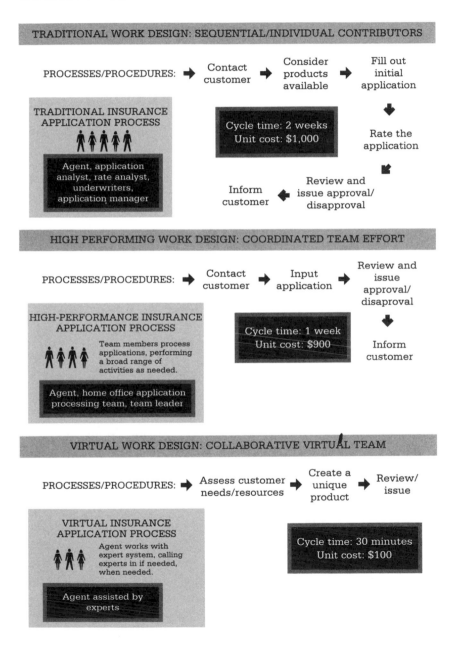

the client's residence. Decisions are made on site. This is possible because all the information, judgment, and decision-making authority are also on site. The skills required by the virtual agent include not only traditional people skills but also computer skills, telecommunication skills, and broader knowledge of insurance products. Rewards programs also will change to provide incentives that are most effective for these employees.

Work Design

Work design is the primary element of workforce effectiveness. It involves the structure of work processes and the definition of work roles. Work design has three components:

1. *People locus*—the activities required to perform the work. It used to matter where people were located. In a virtual workplace, "where" is stretched beyond face-to-face relationships. The correct question is: To what extent can people be provided access to the process, regardless of where they are?

2. *Decision locus*—the kinds of decisions people must make to function. In the virtual workplace, it is important to ask, How can decisions be obtained on demand? What elimination of time and distance is required?

3. *Information locus*—the timing and kinds of information required to make decisions. In the virtual workplace, massive databases are commonplace. The major issue for workforce effectiveness is, How can all conceivably needed information be made accessible to all network participants 24 hours a day?

As shown in Figure 2.10, people in a traditional workplace generally work at a common site with a high division of labor, performing repetitive work. This approach, born in the Industrial Revolution and driven by the bureaucratic model, is aimed at achieving low labor cost. Decisions are made "top-down," and requisite layers of organization drive the decision process. The decision process is supported (or bound) by a highly structured set of protocols, which tend to freeze the long cycle time. Finally, information is guarded, and data that do not support protocols are not necessarily desirable if they upset the routine. Traditional organizations supporting this work process are structured around departments and functions.

The traditional model has evolved into a high-performance or *lean* model, which is characterized by striking differences in the people, decision-making, and information loci. First, there is a reversal of division of labor; teams are used to perform work. Instead of a functional or departmental focus, work is organized around key processes, with individual team members develop-

Figure 2.10 Work Design for Traditional vs. High-Performance vs. Virtual Organizations

Element of Work Design	Traditional	High-Performance	Virtual
People locus	• Low direct labor costs	• Higher direct labor cost	• Moderate direct labor cost
	• High division of labor with low task variety	• Little division of labor with much task variety	• Moderate division of labor with much task variety
	• Individual contribution	• Teams	• Individual contributors/ team combination
	• Work defined by function on a common site	• Work defined by process on a common site	• Work defined by processes and products that transcend the boundary of the organization

(continues)

Figure 2.10 (*continued*)

Element of Work Design	Traditional	High-Performance	Virtual
Decision locus	• Bound by procedures and protocols	• Fewer procedures	• Fewer procedures
	• Managed top-down	• Self-managed teams	• Individual decisions aided by expert systems
	• Long cycle time	• Short cycle time	• Instantaneous cycle time
Information locus	• Information available on a need-to-know basis	• Broad availability of information to support problem-solving efforts	• Information on all aspects of the design, development and distribution process available to entire network

ing multiple skills. Direct labor cost increases on a per-head basis primarily due to this requirement of individual versatility. However, work is still performed on a common site because project work teams require significant interaction to achieve effective results. The overall objective of the high-performance/lean model is to reduce cycle time. There have been hundreds of successful applications of this model, ranging from durable goods manufacturing to insurance operations and consumer customer service operations. To reduce cycle time, these organizations reduce the number of procedures and focus on decision-making at the team level, cutting out numerous bureaucratic layers. Information must be broadly available to support problem solving and decision-making.

The virtual workplace is defined by the process and the product, and it includes the chain of suppliers, purchasers, and manufacturers. It also may rely on significant information databases and transmission capabilities. More specialists will be required in the virtual workplace than in the high-performance organization. These specialists will be available to the virtual network on an on-demand basis. They will be connected to the organization in a number of ways, ranging from the helpline support personnel of computer software companies to computer-network access arrangements.

Note that the virtual workplace does not represent a return to a traditional division of labor and traditional jobs. The virtual work process facilitates more individual contributions on demand from contributors inside and outside the organization. Direct labor costs will be lower than for the high-performance organization because more flexible work arrangements will replace some regular employment.

Skills and Competencies

The virtual workplace will require a highly customized set of skills, ranging from technical specialties to the capacity to work independently in a network or on a string of virtual teams. As with work design, virtual skills and competencies differ from those of high-performance organizations. (See Figure 2.11.)

The skill sets used in the high-performance organization support the centralized role of teams. To operate effectively in project and natural common-site teams, specific skill sets for each member include technical skills, support skills (including those that bridge departments and functions), and team skills (including those required as effective members and leaders). Career paths are defined clearly, and all team members are required to function fully in their role.

The virtual workplace differs in significant ways. The skill sets required are not as stable and predictable as those of high-performance work teams. Specialization is at a premium, but it

Figure 2.11 Skills and Competencies for Traditional vs.
High-Performance vs. Virtual Organizations

Skills and Competencies	Traditional	High-Performance	Virtual
Required skill sets	Each person focuses on his or her own function, segregated by port of entry	Bridge gaps of skill worlds; focus on multi-skilling and versatility	Highly specialized, but must be capable of operating in VR (new skills)
Career path	Rationed by the "pyramid" organization	Clearly structured; each team member is required to fulfill a role on the team	Individual is much more involved on own; career path may traverse traditional boundaries; independent contracting is commonplace
Role of team	Secondary role to support individual contribution	Central to getting work done	A necessity, but much maintenance of team and team management disappears in a VR environment

is not needed all the time. When a special skill is required, the individual must be able to operate as a member of a virtual team. Virtual team skills include a unique combination of cooperative problem-solving behaviors that can be accomplished without being there. A substantial amount of self-management and discipline is also required to accomplish tasks on a timely basis at remote locations (see sidebar 2.3).

2.3   Borg-Warner: Lawyers and Legal Skills on Virtual Teams

Virtual teams derive their advantage from the fact that each member contributes a special skill to the team. In fact, a virtual team finds the best members for a task, no matter where they are.

The law department at Borg-Warner Corp. has been decentralized and distributed across the company. This has allowed the department's role to become much more interactive and constructive. Instead of reviewing projects, members of the department participate in the creation of projects. The department's objective has changed from being a "lawyer bank" that is called on to review projects to an operation that practices preventive law.

Not surprisingly, managers feel more enthusiastic about their own decisions because of their reduced fear of litigation. It is much easier to alter projects to reduce litigation risk during development than to try to convince managers to change a finished project.

(Keith D. Schulz, "Put Your Corporate Counsel Where Your Business Is," *Harvard Business Review*. May/June 1990, 72.)

The career path for the virtual workplace can take three directions:

1. *Traditional career paths.* Some organizations will attempt to provide traditional careers, including hierarchical promotions

for skill and authority. This creates strain on individuals who are working on a team involving members from more than one company to produce a virtual product.

2. *Employment within joint-venture or partnership operations.* The second path, in response to a multiple-company role, is to create new entities, such as joint ventures and partnerships, and to place employees in such organizations. This approach has been used in the cable/telecommunications business. Under the umbrella of a company such as TCI are numerous entities that focus on specific products and markets.[6] The role of each individual is shaped largely by the product subspecialty.

3. *Flexible employment arrangements.* The third path follows the approach of third party contractors who support core employees and work for an organization either for a short period of time or on an on-call basis.

Rewards

Rewards systems include elements of base pay and pay progression, which most often is delivered in the form of merit pay; various forms of contingent compensation; forms of recognition; and health and welfare benefits.

All these elements of rewards systems will undergo change in the virtual workplace. (See Figure 2.12.) Base pay and pay progression will be a less prominent part of the rewards system. People will be less focused on a long-term relationship with their employer and more concerned with the virtual organization—i.e., the tethering of suppliers, producers, and purchasers. Because individuals will begin to concentrate on the value of each virtual interaction, remuneration increasingly will take the form of contract wages and salaries, commissions, and other types of contingent rewards. The temporary nature of the employment relationship will drive more temporary compensation arrangements.

Employers will be faced with a dilemma. On the one hand,

Figure 2.12 Rewards for Traditional vs.
High-Performance vs. Virtual Organizations

Rewards	Traditional	High-Performance	Virtual
Base pay and pay progression	Grade structure/merit pay	Skill-based	Lower prominence of base pay in the total compensation mix
Variable pay	To top of organization only	Broad-based, including goal sharing	Greater focus on commission/ contingency pay
Recognition	Minimal use	Broad-based	Peer recognition and acknowledgment on VR network
Benefits	Noncontributory	Contributory	Self-supplied

employment relationships will be temporary or short-term. However, it will still be necessary for employers to maintain the skills and competencies of the workforce. "Skill-based" contingent pay arrangements will have to be developed that price each contract according to the skills and value involved with the work requirements (see sidebar 2.4). Recognition will be a more natural part of the virtual workplace. Peers will share information, feedback, and performance appraisals as a means of maintaining and upgrading the quality of virtual products and services. Also, as work arrangements grow increasingly flexible, benefits will move more toward being self-supplied.

2.4 Taco Bell: A Highly Leveraged Rewards System

Taco Bell Corp. recently revamped its pay system to include highly leveraged variable pay. For example, the company will not pay people a $50,000 base salary without considering performance, but it will pay a $20,000 bonus on top of a $30,000 base. About 70 percent of the managers receive two-thirds of the maximum bonus or more.

The key to the new system is that the bonus is more performance-oriented. Previously, the company awarded a bonus of $1,000 that was paid out four times a year. Eighty-five percent of the managers received it, and it was a given that the bonus would be awarded if constant performance was maintained.

(Shari Caudron, "Variable-Pay Program Increases Taco Bell's Profits," *Personnel Journal*. June 1993, 64.)

Exploring Work and Rewards in the Virtual Workplace

The technology that has made the virtual organization possible has only begun to be tapped. Our eyes are open wide in wonder and we eagerly anticipate the breakthroughs yet to come. The value of these high-tech miracles, however, will only be as substantial as our ability to implement them within our organizations. Fully as important as the technology is the workforce that uses it. How the components of workforce effectiveness—work design, skills, rewards—are structured will determine an organization's success in the marketplace. Next, we move on to explore the work design that is the foundation for the virtual workplace.

Notes

1. Howard Reingold, *Virtual Reality*. New York: Touchstone/Simon & Schuster, 1991.

2. William H. Davidow and Michael S. Malone, *The Virtual Corporation*. New York: HarperCollins, 1992.

3. N. Fredric Crandall, Marc J. Wallace, Jr., and John Bremen, "Restructuring Rewards for High Performance Organization," *Compensation Guide*. Boston: Warren, Gorham & Lamont, 1997.

4. William Neikirk, "Wanted: Skilled Jack-of-All-Trades," *Chicago Tribune*. February 22, 1993, A1.

5. Marc J. Wallace, Jr., and N. Fredric Crandall, "Winning in the Age of Execution: The Central Role of Workforce Effectiveness," *ACA Journal*. Winter 1992/93, 30–47.

6. Dennis Kneale, Johnnie Roberts, and Laura Landra, "Bell Atlantic and TCI Are Poised to Shape New Interactive World," *The Wall Street Journal*. October 14, 1993, A1.

3

Exploring the Virtual Workplace

Companies adopting the virtual workplace have changed their organizations to create an effective alignment between strategy and work and rewards. There are three models.

The Telecommuting Workplace

Telecommuting is any arrangement, formal or informal, that traditionally employed individuals have with their employer that enables them to work from their home, a telecommuting center, or a satellite office on an occasional or regular basis. Typically, that means anywhere from one to three days a week. For very progressive organizations, however, it can mean five days a week, every week.

The Two Phases of Telecommuting

There are currently two phases of this virtual workplace. Organizations in Phase I are experimenting with telecommuting because employees have requested that they do so. These companies are allowing a handful of individual employees—or specific groups of workers—to work from home or from a telecommuting center or satellite office once or twice a week. Organizations in Phase II of the telecommuting workplace are experimenting with telecommuting because senior management has determined that it makes good business sense. These organizations are willing to consider five-day-a-week telecommuting arrangements—and other types of alternative work systems, and are interested in implementing this virtual workplace corporate-wide.

Phase I of the telecommuting workplace, the more common of the two, can be a dead end because the experimenters are thinking only in terms of today. They typically offer this "flexible" work arrangement only to individual employees who've requested it, and they consider the arrangement to be a "benefit" they're providing employees. Because these organizations consider telecommuting to be an infrequently offered employee benefit, applications of the workplace are small and scattered, quietly implemented, undocumented, and unleveraged. When the telecommuter quits or retires, the telecommuting arrangement is also retired. The strategic implications of the workplace—and its bottom-line benefits to the company—are neither recognized nor studied.

A Brief History

Historically, the telecommuting movement has been driven by employees, not by senior management. Larry Barrett, managing director of the International Teleconferencing Association's Telecommuting and Telework Division in McLean, Virginia, notes that "employees hear about it, investigate it, and collectively put pressure on human resources or alternative work arrangement management to do it." As a bottom-up movement, traditional telecommuting arrangements—doled out as a 'benefit' to employees—have not saved or generated significant amounts of money.

Telecommuters are typically employees who have been with a company for a while and have a need for increased flexibility in their work arrangements. Sometimes, they need flexibility to manage a caregiving situation; other times, there's a need to meet deadlines and be able to work for long, uninterrupted periods. Still other times, as at the GTE Corporation, a telecommuting situation arises from a highly valued employee's wish to continue working with the company in spite of a spouse's relocation. "We have a very outstanding employee who said, 'If I couldn't telecommute, I couldn't do my job with GTE,'" relays Francine Riley, retired director of workforce diversity with the Stamford, Connecticut-based telecommunications company, and manager of several telecommuters.

> "She loves her job, and she loves her husband and family; but they live out on a farm, and she has a couple of hours' commute each way. Her husband farms and works a second job until 11:30 P.M. Now, the employee works from home three days a week, and she and her son and her husband have time together in the morning."

Telecommuting was a way for this longtime employee to keep her job. It was also a way for GTE to retain a highly valued employee. Says Riley, "Telecommuting allows her to lead the life she wants to where she wants to and still do her job."

Most telecommuters work at home or at a satellite office or telecommuting center between one and three days a week. However, there are certain interactions that need to be handled in person. Faxes and conference calls don't replace human contact, the absence of which can reduce relationships and human trust. In fact, building trust between managers and employees is one of the biggest challenges in implementing a telecommuting program. Managers who are accustomed to managing by walking around and observing employees are suddenly faced with a dilemma: How can I manage what I can't see? And, if I do let him stay home, he may cheat me and the company out of time and work! The thing to remember here is that effective management doesn't come only from face-to-face contact; it comes from an employee's sense of personal ownership of the business process and its results. A manager should work with employees until they take personal ownership of their jobs and feel rewarded by getting work done on time.

Other common challenges to telecommuting include:

• *Communication.* Managers and employees are afraid of losing the informal, "water-cooler" conversations they've come to take for granted, and the open-door office policy that enables them to interrupt anybody anytime. These informal communications methods need to be replaced, to some degree, by regular, scheduled telephone conversations, e-mail communication, and periodic, scheduled, face-to-face meetings. Telecommuting and other virtual workplace arrangements suffer most from people's inability to structure communications efforts that have always been taken care of informally (and not necessarily well), and to use the technology that's available to keep the lines of communication open and flowing both ways.

• *Measuring work by standards other than time.* Telecommuters' work must be evaluated in terms of measurable standards, such as their ability to meet project goals and deadlines and produce work that meets predetermined quality standards. Telecommuting should be supported by a performance management program that defines performance and development objectives and measurements up front and then uses e-mail, telephone, fax, and face-to-face meetings to provide ongoing coaching and feedback.

• *Maintaining and supporting teams.* Just because some employees are off-site occasionally or permanently doesn't mean work teams can't thrive. Teams, like individuals, can communicate via electronic media, meet regularly face to face, pass work around via electronic media, and talk on the telephone.

• *The legal issues: Where does the workplace begin and end?* Consultants and association executives say the legal issue of corporate liability is no higher in a home office than in a corporate office. "The fears raised are far out of proportion to reality," asserts Gil Gordon, a telecommuting expert. "It's a minimal risk that can be very well managed using common sense." Elaine Fox, a labor attorney with D'Ancona & Pflaum in Chicago, agrees. "A lot of this is quickly evolving. I don't think there's been any definition of where the workplace really is."

• *Union opposition.* It may be difficult to overcome union opposition to telecommuting, since unions still remember the abusive practices of "homework" suffered largely by immigrant women in the early days of New York's garment industry. Unions also have another reason for opposing off-site work: Employees who work off site in their own private offices are more difficult to organize. Our suggestion to union officials is this: Recognize that virtual organizations are here to stay and find different ways to communicate with members and prospective members. Remember, there's little risk of employees suffering at the hands of employers who force them into telecommuting relationships. Most often, these work arrangements are offered to salaried employees provided with full benefits who are empowered to do their jobs and generally set their own hours.

• *Coping with the Fair Labor Standards Act (FLSA) of 1938.* Though this act has strict provisions about overtime compensation, time can be tracked off-site in the same way as in the office, by having employees enter their time on a time sheet or computer system.

The Real Estate Factor

Strategically, companies are beginning to look increasingly at telecommuting programs for cost savings and revenue generation. Real estate savings comes when companies cut the ratio of physical workstations to employees. Traditionally, the ratio of workstations to employees has been 1:1; in other words, one employee to one workstation. Now, some companies are shifting the ratio to 1:5 and even 1:10. This is being accomplished through systems like shared officing, or *hoteling*. Through a hoteling system, employees reserve space when they know they'll be in the office. That means a telecommuter with a fixed schedule might reserve an office for use every Monday, Tuesday, and Friday. The office or workspace the telecommuter uses each time might be different, but the facilities—a computer, a telephone, a fax machine, a copy machine, a modem, etc.—remain constant. A telecommuter with a flexible schedule would have to reserve space ahead of time when he or she plans a trip to the office.

The concept of *shared officing* is a less drastic way to reduce the physical space in the office. It gives employees a bit more of that comfortable, traditional feeling of "spatial ownership" than does hoteling. Organizations that employ the concept of shared officing might arrange for two or more employees to share a given workspace, each coming to the office at different times during the week to use it.

These arrangements have quite an impact on the bottom line. Michael Bell, a telecommuting real estate expert for Dun & Bradstreet, notes:

> "Most organizations think in terms of 220 to 300 gross square feet per employee when they rent or buy office space. In the U. S., central district office space costs an average of $20 per square foot. That means companies are spending about $4,400 (a conservative estimate) per employee for physical space alone. When you consider the cost of ancillary support systems (technology, office support, etc.), which average between $8,000 to $10,000 per employee per year, you're talking about minimum spatial costs of about $14,440 annually per employee—a hefty chunk of change. Using hoteling systems, shared officing, and other virtual workplace arrangements, virtual companies like IBM, AT&T, Andersen Consulting, and Hewlett-Packard are able to achieve roughly 35 to 55 percent reductions in space."

A Telecommuting Case Study

The way GTE Corporation's telecommuting policy got started is typical of the launch of employee-driven programs. There, recalls Riley, telecommuting was a "desperation move."

> "I had a fairly large staff, and one of my people was getting married. I was going to lose her because her husband-to-be lived one hundred miles away. I didn't want to lose her; we were going through downsizing and job freezes, and I knew I wouldn't be able to re-place her. The telecommuting arrangement was really a desperation move. One of the staff engineers came up with an idea for her to work from home a few days a week, with a computer and fax . . . he said it would be seamless, that people wouldn't even know where she was working from.
>
> "We hooked up the lines and went through a num-ber of agreements discussing how it would work, what days she would be in, when she would work from home, and so forth. I got permission from my boss—I was nervous and so was he—and we decided to try it for six months. It took us five to six weeks to get the wrinkles out and work things smoothly in terms of communication . . . and it worked so smoothly that, when the next person came to me from the staff and needed a flexible work arrangement, we were quick to try this again. Pretty soon we had six people working in flexible work arrangements."

People in other divisions of GTE heard about what Riley's department was doing and wanted to learn how to construct sim-ilar telecommuting arrangements in their own divisions. Once es-tablished in her role as director of diversity, Riley and her staff made a videotape detailing their alternative work arrangements.

Employee interest in telecommuting at GTE continued to build; an employee involvement group in the Texas facility discussed it over the computer lines. The heightened interest coincided with a request for help made by the Dallas Department of Transportation (DDOT). The DDOT wanted corporate volunteers to participate in a pilot program to test the theory that telecommuting could significantly reduce traffic and benefit the environment. GTE's Texas facility offered to be part of the telecommuting pilot.

Through the program, one hundred twenty salaried employees worked from home one day a week for six months, on either Tuesday, Wednesday, or Thursday. GTE took the opportunity afforded by the pilot to measure absenteeism, turnover, productivity, turnaround time to customers, supervisory challenges, and more. "We were elated with the results [of the pilot]," says Riley. "Motivation went up, and productivity went up 15 to 20 percent—and that's a conservative figure," she adds. "People told us they took enough work home for the day and were finished by noon because they had no interruptions."

Culture Shift

As the GTE example illustrates, telecommuting programs launch major culture shifts for organizations. Organizations that traditionally manage by walking around have to learn to manage by results. Similarly, traditional communications methods, like physical memos and sitting down together over a cup of coffee, are challenged, and previously unconscious processes are made conscious and intentional.

Most of all, the focus of work begins to shift away from internally focused processes and time-based measurement standards and toward the customer and results-based measurement standards. That's the beginning of an important shift in corporate focus from internal events, like work flow, to external results, like turnaround time to the customer. These results become increasingly tied to the customer as the level of virtualness in the organization increases. This culture shift doesn't happen overnight. It's driven by changes in technology, increasing employee empowerment and the knowledge that success is dependent on the degree to which customers are satisfied.

To a large extent, it's also driven by employee selection and training. A newly-launched telecommuting program works best if the people in it—managers and employees—are "virtual pioneers." These are the people who want to change the way they work, who are excited by technology, and who strive for flexibility in their work arrangements. Virtual pioneers can also be people who:

- Are willing to participate by necessity. For example, a young mother who has to balance the duties of raising a two-year-old with the responsibilities of her job might look to telecommuting as the only way she can "do it all."
- Understand and are interested in adopting new information technology.
- Have a tolerance for change.
- Are able to relate to "process" as opposed to "function" or "occupation."
- Are not locked into years of thinking and doing things in only one way.

Managers who micromanage, look over people's shoulders, and don't trust employees won't be able to manage telecommuters or other employees in the virtual workplace, so select these people right out. Managers who thrive in the virtual environment routinely train, develop, and trust employees, and manage for results.

Once you have selected supervisors you expect to be successful telemanagers, you might consider training them. "Supervisor training for telecommuting is a must," asserts Gil Gordon.

"We've seen clearly the difference between companies that have provided training and those that haven't. Providing training changes the experience from being one of 'trial and error' to being one of 'trial and success.' There's nothing in the training that's new, but providing it short-cuts the learning process. It enables people to go into the telecommuting program with confidence."

Supervisors should be trained in using the new technology. They should also consider what Gordon calls a "refresher course" in how to be a good manager: preferably one that reinforces skills such as setting clear performance and results goals, monitoring performance and results, and providing ongoing feedback. Managers may also need to learn how to keep telecommuters linked to the office and how to act as a communications link between the remote workforce and the office.

It's just as important to select and train *telecommuters* you expect to be successful in the new environment. Telecommuting isn't for everyone. First of all, not everyone wants to set up an office in their home; some people want work to be left at work and home to be left at home. And telecommuting centers may not be right for all people either; not every employee is suited to telework, or any kind of remote work, for that matter. The people you select to help launch your telecommuting should be proven self-starters. They should also be able and willing to work independently; be self-motivated; be creative thinkers who are able to perceive hurdles and overcome them; produce high-quality work; and be good communicators.

For telecommuters, training should cover technology as well as the ins and outs of setting up a business from home, including issues of safety, ergonomics, and boundaries between work life and non-work life. Because they're functioning as mini-businesses that represent your organization, they should also be thoroughly schooled in:

• *The business*. In a remote office, it's more difficult to put a caller on hold and check basic business facts. Employees should know the fundamental economics of their business, as well as key facts about their customers and their operations.

• *Performance management skills*. Performance management, particularly in the virtual workplace, is a two-way street. Employees, as well as supervisors, have to learn how to set goals and give and receive feedback.

• *Being a member of a virtual team.* Teamwork is more important and more challenging when physical contact is limited. Employees need to learn how to communicate effectively using e-mail, telephones, faxes, modems, and scheduled face-to-face meetings.

Implementing the Telecommuting Workplace

Whether you're interested in offering employees a one-day-a-week telecommuting option or a five-day-a-week option, we suggest you follow these five steps (see Figure 3.1).:

1. *Define your organization's need for virtual solutions.* It's important to identify your organization's reasons for considering a telecommuting or other virtual workplace program. Are you trying to offer flexible work alternatives to employees? Or is your objective cost containment or a reduction in turnover or absenteeism? As you examine your reasons for considering telecommuting, make an effort to look down the road five to ten years. You may have an interest in telecommuting as the first in a series

Figure 3.1 Implementing the Telecommuting Workplace

1. Define your organization's need for virtual solutions.
2. Analyze work in your organization to determine which activities and projects might be done remotely.
3. Identify virtual pioneers.
4. Provide employees with the freedom to create work arrangements that make sense to them.
5. Get employees past the novelty of their new work arrangements and focused on their work.

of virtual steps you're going to take to get ahead and stay ahead of the competition. How will you decide? First, do a needs analysis that assesses the interest, flexibility, willingness, and readiness of your employees, managers, and customers to "go virtual." In your survey, be sure to ask people what they see their organization's work arrangements looking like in five years. Be sure, also, that you've defined clearly what telecommuting is, and what other virtual workplaces—like the frontline and the cyberlink models—look like, so employees and managers can think in terms of where telecommuting might lead your organization.

2. *Analyze work in your organization to determine which activities and projects might be done remotely.* Once you've identified the activities in your organization that might be done remotely, set up measurement systems and processes that will help supervisors and employees know what's expected of them. Have parameters within which to work and manage for results. For example, a telemarketer might be expected to make fifty calls per day; a public relations employee might be deemed successful if he or she produces three press releases a week and places six articles a month. Let the work specifications and the employees doing the jobs help you establish fair, accurate systems for remotely measuring progress and results.

3. *Identify virtual pioneers.* As we mentioned earlier, virtual pioneers—both employees and managers—are the people in your organization who have a real, personal interest in virtual work arrangements and systems. Identify these people in your organization through your needs analysis survey instrument, a separate survey instrument, or an e-mail or bulletin board 'call' for virtual volunteers. Once you've identified these people in your organization (hopefully, the majority of them have identified themselves), encourage them to get out of the office, visit customer sites, and learn how to make their jobs more customer-responsive. Your entrance into the virtual workplace is your organization's opportunity to change the way it does business to be more customer-focused and customer-responsive. Have your

virtual pioneers think of ways to redesign their jobs in the office and away from the office to be more customer-oriented, efficient, and productive. Encourage them to visit other companies that have telecommuting or more advanced virtual workplace arrangements that you and your organization can learn from.

4. *Provide employees with the freedom to create work arrangements that make sense to them—to do whatever is needed to operate an office away from the physical office.* At this stage, most companies will either ask employees to tell them what equipment and supplies they need to do their job remotely or leave it to them to stock supplies and equipment. Whether or not your organization purchases and sets up all of the home-office equipment needed—computer hardware, software, extra telephone lines, modem, fax modem or machine, scanner, printer, and other essentials—depends on the scope of your telecommuting program, how much equipment participating employees already have in place, equipment standardization issues, and so forth. Says GTE's Riley:

"In the telepilot in Dallas, we found that most people had computers at home. . . . Some did not, and those that did not, we got computers to them . . . we [also] found in Dallas that some people were happy to pay for the extra necessities of telecommuting because they were thrilled to work from home. There's also the savings to consider for employees, such as the costs of commuting, the wear and tear on the car, dry cleaning costs, food costs, etc."

5. *Get employees past the novelty of the technology and their new work arrangements and focused on work.* Telecommuting is a big change for your organization and employees, and it's going to take some time to adjust. Once the technological bugs are worked out of the system and everyone settles into the new routine—usually five to six weeks—customer satisfaction should once again be the focus of work.

The Frontline Workplace

For customers, on-time, online service translates into more face-to-face interaction with service providers and more client-needs-centered assistance. This type of service is of far greater value to customers than the traditional segmented sales and service approach. It is delivered by people who know what their clients want because they often work on the job with the client in the client's own place of business.

But what does it mean for organizations? For one thing, it means seriously leveraging technology to maximize their use of people. They're moving sales and service frontline employees out of the office and into the field to work from remote locations, mobile offices, customer locations, and just about anywhere else. They're cutting real estate costs and adding some technological ones. Most importantly, they're realizing significant boosts in customer satisfaction and retention *and* employee satisfaction and performance, and those results alone, though difficult to quantify, are worth the costs associated with the workforce shift.

A Frontline Case Study: IBM

"In the early '90s," says Andréa J. Cheatham, a business unit executive with IBM's Workforce Mobility Transformation Services and the former project manager for IBM's first virtual office, "we started looking at how we might enhance overall customer satisfaction and employee productivity." At the same time, she continues, "we had a real estate consideration: Our lease was about to expire. In questioning whether we really needed another big office, we realized that, with one of our goals being to increase face-to-face customer contact, the answer was 'no.' "

IBM decided to experiment with ways to reduce the need for sales and service employees to come into the office. It launched the first pilot of its now widespread Mobility virtual office program in 1992, in the company's Norfolk, Virginia, marketing and service office. The initial switch to the virtual environment involved fifty-eight marketing and service employees and took about eight months to implement. Hallmarks of the program included workspace sharing, increased face time with customers, and decreased cycle time to get information back to the customer.

The pilot was so successful that requests for similar arrangements came pouring in from IBM sales offices nationwide. Employees loved Mobility because of the flexibility and customers loved it because their sales and service representatives were immediately more tuned in to their needs and more responsive. In fact, customer response has been so positive that, in 1995, IBM decided to launch a consulting service aimed at helping its customers make their own conversion to a virtual office environment.

Today, over 20,000 employees in IBM's national sales force operate within the context of the frontline arrangement. The result? By implementing a shared office plan with a 10:1 ratio of employees to office space, the company has reduced its real estate requirements by 40 to 60 percent across the country. It has also increased employee productivity by 15 percent in two years and increased customer face time by six hours per employee per week.

While some companies hand imperatives down from the top, IBM decided on a high employee involvement approach. For the pilot, says Cheatham, "We pulled together a cross-functional team of employees within the [Norfolk] office . . . and conducted an electronic brainstorming session aimed at addressing customer satisfaction, employee productivity, and real estate concerns." Right away the team decided that a bigger office wasn't the answer to the company's problems. Instead, it determined, the company could increase customer face time and hopefully increase employee productivity by shifting employees' focus from the physical office to the customer site. That meant packing employees up and getting them on the road.

To that end, IBM equipped sales and service personnel with the appropriate package of technology tools and developed a support structure back at the office to help off-site employees secure the additional assistance they might need. By fully equipping employees with the latest technology, IBM relieved its sales force of the need to travel to the office for other than just housekeeping matters. Sales and service employees participating in the pilot were able to use the company's technologies—the same solutions they were marketing to customers—to answer customers' questions and take care of business wherever they were: . . . at a customer site, in an airport, or at home.

Both the remote work arrangements and the team planning concept worked well for IBM. For that reason, as the Mobility program was extended to other sales and service sites nationwide, a second cross-functional team of employees was assembled to head the implementation.

One key to the program's success, suggests Cheatham, is "meticulous" documentation. "IBM has produced an extensive manual that covers every conceivable aspect of a conversion to a virtual office," she says. The manual is the result of brainstorming and planning efforts of representatives from seven disciplines within the organization: human resources, telephone systems, technology, real estate, the legal department, business planning, and process planning.

A standardized course of training helps get all employees off to a good start in the virtual environment. The company introduces employees to the new work arrangement through a four- to six-hour course of instruction. Among other things, employees are taught to use a laptop computer and to access information remotely. In anticipation of questions that might arise regarding the technology they're given to work with, IBM equipped its laptops with a plethora of "most commonly asked" questions and answers.

Communication, too, has become more structured—in a flexible way. Because people are in different places at different times, more forethought has had to be given to the need to meet on a regular basis to touch base and share experiences. Possible locations for meetings, however, have broadened considerably. Says Cheatham, "Prior to the advent of the virtual sales office, teams were convened regularly in centralized spots around the country for local, regional, and national meetings. These days, by contrast, managers are more likely to conduct their staff meetings in flexible locations: restaurants, hotels, and even customer sites." IBM also makes use of tele- and videoconferencing modes of communication, says Cheatham. "People have learned to compensate. They don't have to have the face-to-face interaction that was once required."

Lessons Learned

Success depends largely on the ability to be flexible and learn from mistakes. Each company must create a program that fits its organization's needs—and modify that program where and when necessary. Experienced frontliners offer these words of wisdom and suggestions:

1. *Beware of some supervisors' tendency to keep managing traditionally, rewarding employees who* appear *to work hard and spend many hours on the job.* To manage successfully in the virtual environment, leaders must have the self-confidence and comfort level needed to challenge employees to do great things—and then get out of their way. They must let their employees determine how best to achieve the goals set before them and manage employee output, not input. Helping managers make the transition from managing by line-of-sight to managing goal attainment and results is a common challenge in this model.

2. *Focus on education.* Employees have different technological and interpersonal skills, and it's difficult to know where training needs lie. Do you need to spend more time training employees to use laptops to remotely access the company's database, or are employees' time management skills poor? Should you devote extra time to partnering with customers? The best way to avoid education and training pitfalls is to do a training needs analysis that involves employees and managers. Develop

an understanding of your workforce's basic training needs first—in *all* areas—and plan to meet more advanced training needs later on.

3. *Offer technological support.* Though most of the companies we've studied have sophisticated technology in place to support their virtual workplace efforts, many still struggle with issues like concurrent, remote requests for data that overload the system and off-site mechanical failures that require immediate attention. At AT&T, for example, it soon became clear that internal operating systems had to be dramatically altered to accommodate the needs of a remote sales force. And when a salesperson in the field has a mechanical problem with his or her equipment, you need to have a support plan in place that enables the sales force to access help immediately when a machine isn't working.

4. *Beware of shallow commitments to virtual work arrangements.* Though virtual arrangements spark enthusiasm at first, particularly in employees, enthusiasm can diminish or die as work roles are redefined and the realities of virtual work—for example, isolation and autonomy—are experienced. Two things must be considered here: (1) It's possible that some of the people who are experiencing a loss of commitment to the virtual work arrangement are simply not cut out for nontraditional work. It requires employees to be highly organized and self-motivated. These employees may be more comfortable in a traditional office setting. (2) For those who work well remotely but don't know how to deal with feelings of isolation, scheduling face-to-face meetings with coworkers and teams, meeting online for a quick chat, and having more frequent conference calls may be helpful.

5. *Keep informal knowledge transfer alive.* When employees work from locations other than the office, opportunities for informal conversation among employees can be limited or lost. That can be a blow to teamwork. It can also mean the end of business opportunities that come from day-to-day networking. But it doesn't have to mean any of that. The key is to replace the "informal" chats with "formal" ones that take place over the In-

ternet, during brown-bag teleconference lunches, and in planned face-to-face meetings on the road. These more formal communications methods, though they seem foreign at first, can actually *increase* knowledge-sharing between larger and more diverse groups of employees.

6. *Ease the paradigm shift caused by sharing office space.* It's easy to disregard the feelings engendered by a loss of spatial ownership in the virtual environment, but those feelings can present challenges. This goes back to the need for effectively dealing with these changes up front and early.

Implementing the Frontline Workplace

In addition to the steps listed under "Implementing the Telecommuting Workplace," the following three steps are recommended (see Figure 3.2):

1. *Develop a frontline infrastructure (work design).* It's important to be as clear as possible about work roles, what's expected of employees, and what support systems are available. Put together a policy that defines the frontline concept for your organization and offers guidelines to supervisors and employees working with each other in this virtual arrangement. Elements of a frontline policy include:

- The definition and interpretation of the frontline workplace for your organization. It's important that you create

Figure 3.2 Implementing the Frontline Workplace

1. Develop a frontline infrastructure (work design).
2. Start systematically tearing down brick and mortar and building virtual systems designed to serve the customer.
3. Shift your culture away from "My supervisor is the boss" to "My customer is the boss."

this definition—and the program itself—specifically for your organization, taking into account its culture and the needs of individual employees and supervisors expected to work together in the virtual arrangement.

- An explanation of the principles of the frontline workplace in your organization. Include statements regarding business needs, terms and conditions of employment, equipment provision, workspace designation, the frontline agreement, tax implications, and scheduling.
- Details about the selection of candidates for the virtual work arrangement. Include a discussion of the job skills and duties, as well as the characteristics you'll be looking for in employees and supervisors involved in the program.
- Information about equipment assignment and upkeep. Employees working in this virtual arrangement will most likely need a variety of technology tools (laptop computer, cellular phone, fax/modem, pager, and a variety of software). Specify here which tools, if any, will be supplied and maintained by the organization, which tools the employee is responsible for, and who will own what if the employment relationship ends.
- An explanation of the process your organization will use to measure employee/supervisor performance and evaluate the success of the program.
- Details on timekeeping. Is it important that employees work a traditional 40 hours a week or more, or are you simply concerned with their output? Discuss these issues in the timekeeping section of your policy, making sure to emphasize changes from your current policy, if there are any, and to state whether or not employees will be compensated for overtime.
- Tips on safety. Since employees will literally be working from anywhere, they may need some help with ergonomics. You may also want to have an agreement with employees that clearly states their responsibility for their own safety and your responsibility for their safety.

2. *Start systematically tearing down brick and mortar and building virtual systems designed to serve the customer.* In the telecommuting workplace, we recommended that virtual work arrangements be optional. At the frontline level, however, the new work arrangements should simply be *the way sales and service are done.* It's true that virtual work isn't for everyone, and organizations should consider redeploying employees and supervisors who are unwilling or unable to adapt to the virtual environment. In order to realize the potential benefits of the frontline arrangement, however, organizations have to be willing to take a stand and stick with it.

3. *Shift the culture away from "My supervisor is the boss" to "My customer is the boss."* For an organization to be successful in its virtual work efforts, it has to wholly embrace the notion of serving the customer. From this point on, then, in your frontline workplace, your customer is the boss. Supervisors and managers are simply there to help guide employees in their efforts to meet the needs of the organization's *ultimate* boss: the customer.

The Cyberlink Workplace

The cyberlink workplace is the most customer-focused embodiment of virtual work. It's found wherever teams involving customers, suppliers, and/or producers form to manage work collaboratively. In a cyberlink workplace, teams of customers, suppliers, and producers work together face to face and in cyberspace to realize a product or service goal. When business opportunities have been fully realized, these teams may disband, and individuals from the team form new teams with other customers, producers, and suppliers to work on other projects.

The cyberlink workplace is more than customer-focused; it's customer-dependent. The goal of the workplace is to capture the hearts and minds of its customers and encourage repeat business, longer-term contracts and, ultimately, ongoing partnerships. With the cyberlink workplace, the customer is a key part of the process of manufacturing goods and delivering services. The customer's needs, goals, and challenges actually drive his or her supplier's business, because customer satisfaction and loyalty are key to corporate survival.

Organizations that implement the cyberlink workplace are truly externally focused. Inside the organization, employees are driven by process, not by function or job title. They work with customers to ensure satisfaction from the beginning of the relationship to the end.

While the cyberlink workplace requires organizations to restructure their cultures and work systems, it yields great results for the effort. Employers who have implemented this type of workplace have seen:

• *A new, corporate-wide focus on speed of execution.* The emphasis on speed can be seen in areas like customer service and new product development, as well as in internal corporate communications.

• *A shared sense of strategy and purpose developing among all employees.* The customer orientation typical of this workplace unites employees and helps bring an organization's vision and values to the foreground.

• *Employees whose jobs have become centered around serving the customer.* They have more clearly articulated roles, responsibilities and accountabilities.

• *The emergence of a truly empowered workforce.* Decision-making shifts from managers and supervisors to employees, who are closest to the customer—around whom work is actually centered.

• *Reward systems that are closely aligned to the company's key strategies, goals, and revenues.* Teams of employees from all areas of the organization are being compensated under such systems.

• *Communication becoming more open, timely, candid, and ongoing—across functions.* This occurs largely as a result of advanced information technology systems (like e-mail, town meetings, groupware, etc.). Customers are often invited to participate in electronic and face-to-face problem-solving sessions.

• *Teams managing and directing themselves.* Fewer managers and supervisors are needed. Team leaders are emerging and acting as facilitators of group problem-solving processes.

• *The electronic sharing of information leading employees, customers, and suppliers to think "outside the box."* Combined with the shift in roles, responsibilities, and work paradigms, this strategy is resulting in new business opportunities, new products, new markets, and new services.

A Cyberlink Workplace Case Study

It's one thing to be closer to the customer, working on-site and really learning his or her business so that you can communicate his or her needs more effectively to your own company. But how does it work when the customer is actually *on* the team—or leading it? This is exactly what Ross Operating Valve Company did. The company's ROSS/FLEX process, a process by which the customer is the lead designer on the team, constitutes a major percentage of its total business, and has helped the company significantly grow its standard business. ROSS/FLEX is a process by which a customer works with an engineer and a vertical specialist (a salesperson/resource person who specializes in a particular industry) to create his or her own valve, specific to the architecture of the machinery that he or she is trying to build or use.

"The design engineer takes the customer's wants and turns them into a product that they can look at together by fax or modem," explains David Ross, director of North American marketing for the manufacturer of pneumatic control valves, based in Troy, Michigan.

"By looking at the envelope or outside designs, the customer can change or reconfigure his prototype at will.

"This market-creating or virtual prototyping piece of our business allows the customer to have what he wants very rapidly. The vertical specialist, design engineer, and customer are working together and are connected intimately throughout the project. Essentially, we are creating products the customer wants virtually at his doorstep, much like one would order a pizza."

Depending on the complexity of the project, it takes Ross engineers two days to a week to develop a prototype the customer can put his or her hands on.

The ROSS/FLEX process was launched in 1990 at the company's Lavonia, Georgia plant.

"The arrangement had its original thinking in Henry Duigman, Ross' former chief operating officer (since retired), who had a vision of manufacturing in America. Duigman felt that customers had limited choices, and that standard manufacturing practices didn't give them what they were looking for . . . It took him a few years to get us turned around from a company that felt 'you can do business with us as long as you do it our way' to a company that was truly customer-focused."

Today, the Ross Valve Company is so customer-focused that the customer is leading the design team. How did the company do it? "There's nothing super-rocket science about it," says Ross. "It's all commercially available equipment, and any good engineering school can produce engineers to man the equipment." The key, he says, is that Ross Valve hires new graduates of engineering schools—individuals with no preconceptions of what it's like to be an engineer and no bias regarding the process by which products are designed. "Even though they have counterparts on the other end of the company who design traditionally, ROSS/FLEX engineers do not design traditionally. They'd be frustrated quickly to work on new standard projects that would take months to develop."

But the company's success is due to more than just strategic hiring, says Ross. "We've invested heavily in efforts to change the culture of marketing, engineering, and manufacturing from individual, separate functions to a holistic approach to doing business," he explains. With that goal in mind, traditional salespeople slated to work within the ROSS/FLEX process traded in their geographic responsibilities for industry-specific ones, based on their own particular interests. "They now have the responsibility and authority to travel wherever their industry requires," says Ross. "By doing this, they become so intimate with their industry and so well-known at customer plants and headquarters that they are widely accepted as experts in the field."

In addition to being encouraged to pursue their industry-specific interests, vertical marketing specialists have been given the opportunity to do what all salespeople dream of: to go out and convince customers that they can have anything they want. "As soon as customers began taking advantage of the process," recalls Ross, "Customers owned it. The 'sale' was over."

To make the ROSS/FLEX process truly holistic, employees from all functions are encouraged to look over each other's shoulders and appreciate the full scope of the projects they undertake. Engineers go on sales calls, salespeople sit in front of engineers' terminals, and machinists sit up with design engineers. This holistic approach, though difficult to achieve, has been proven to work well inside and outside the company.

> "If you connect the three parties—the customer, the vertical marketing specialist and the engineer—the relationship is better than if you insulate and isolate the three parties. When the customer is isolated, he has no one to feel close with. He can only look at the end result, and he doesn't see and understand the value of the product that was produced for him. He thinks it's something he has to shop around and compare to.

When the customer is integrated, he knows his ideas
are being passed to an engineer and he has ownership
of the project."

Because it integrates advanced technology with people from
the customer, supplier, and producer, the cyberlink model has
reaped magnificent rewards for manufacturing and service organizations nationwide.

Speed and efficiency, as Ross Valve Company has discovered, leads to deeper, better relationships with customers. The
ROSS/FLEX process, however, has also directly benefited the
bottom line. It has given the company, among other things, a research and development division that is supported by customers
(since some of the customer-designed products go on to become
standard offerings at the pneumatic valve company) and a business on top of their off-the-shelf product line.

Implementing the Cyberlink Workplace

Of course, making the transition from a traditional workplace to a cyberlink workplace isn't easy. It calls for a complete
cultural overhaul—one that looks closely at the way work systems and jobs are structured and at the way individuals are
compensated. Cyberlink workplaces look different from organization to organization. Some arrangements involve teams of customers, producers and suppliers. Others involve long-term
customer/supplier partnerships that change the way work is
done within one or both of the organizations.

In addition to the steps suggested in association with the
implementation of telecommuting and frontline workplaces,
here are three additional steps (see Figure 3.3).:

1. *Broaden cyberspace to include customers and suppliers.* Work
as a team to invent, design, and produce new products and services. Your new boss is the customer, and you, as the customer,
are your suppliers' "boss." It's perfectly natural, then, that you
talk about your needs and concerns, your customers' needs and

Figure 3.3 Implementing the Cyberlink Workplace

1. Broaden cyberspace so that you include customers and suppliers.

2. Subcontract (outsource) all work that doesn't support your company's strategic effort.

3. Reconstruct all work systems around virtual reality.

concerns, and your suppliers' needs and concerns, and that you identify areas in which your challenges and solutions overlap. After you've made a commitment to work as a team for as long as it takes to realize business opportunities, don't underestimate how much time it will take to work out the bugs in technology and human interaction. You'll have a better chance at success if each member of the team defines his or her priorities and values, both in terms of what each wants to accomplish and how he or she wants to accomplish it, early in the relationship. No matter how great the technology is, this needs to happen. The "how we work together" is just as important as the "what we produce."

2. *Subcontract (outsource) all work that doesn't support your company's strategic effort.* This includes all work in which your company doesn't have a competitive advantage, such as payroll processing, building maintenance and cleaning, and billing. Continuing to do unrelated jobs, like payroll processing and building maintenance, won't help you achieve your goal of being the best manufacturer of control valves in the business. It also won't help you woo and support customers, or be in touch with their needs.

3. *Reconstruct all work systems around virtual reality.* At this level, bricks and mortar are not central to business; they are simply tools to help you invent, design, and produce high-quality products and services quickly and efficiently.

The Virtual Workplace: What We Have Learned

The virtual workplace, by definition, is in continual transformation. The unprecedented pace of technological change constantly introduces new opportunities to seize competitive advantage. The pace of organizational change, although accelerating, is much slower, and is fraught with barriers of human adaptability to change itself. Thus, our caution that you may not necessarily move through the stages of telecommuting and the frontline model to the cyberlink workplace takes on a harder edge—you may not have a choice!

We will methodically progress through the elements of the virtual workplace related to work design, skills and competencies, and rewards in the following chapters. At the same time, we will outline our insights into the New Deal, which provides a path for implementing the important aspects of the human side of these changes.

4

Work Design

Work design arranges the things people do on the job. Assembly line workers assembling automobiles are working within a work design. Surgeons, nurses, and medical technicians performing open heart surgery; sales representatives engaged in winning a sale; college professors addressing a class; and policemen directing traffic are all engaged in work. Work design, then, refers to the structuring of work—what people actually do, the decisions they make, and the knowledge, skills, and experience they need to succeed.

Work design is of critical concern for managers because it bears directly on performance. How a company arranges work has a direct bearing on productivity, quality, cost, profits, and customer satisfaction. Achieving dramatic improvements in these measures in virtual work settings demands rethinking traditional notions of work. This chapter explores the changes required in moving from traditional arrangements to virtual work designs and the role of work design in the virtual workplace. First, we will define work design and why it is important. Then we will examine the major dimensions of work design by using several examples of actual companies. We will also show how virtual work designs differ from traditional work designs. We will then explore how to make the transition from traditional to virtual work designs. Finally, we will see how teams must develop and evolve for virtual work designs to achieve results.

The West Bend Story

The West Bend Company's Beverage Maker Division[1] provides a dramatic case of how work design must change in order for the virtual organization to succeed. In the early '90s the company faced a crisis encountered frequently in our economy: customers revolted. A majority of the company's product sales (beverage makers) were concentrated with four or five big customers (Wal-Mart, Kmart, and Price Club, for example) and all were demanding the following concessions from West Bend to continue doing business:

1. Certify 100 percent quality of products coming into the retailer's system.
2. Deliver in small, not large, lot sizes (to minimize in-store inventory).
3. Cut delivery time from two weeks to 24 hours (to serve just-in-time inventory goals).
4. Reduce product cost dramatically—by at least 20 percent.

Traditional manufacturers would protest that these retailers were asking for the impossible in the form of perfect quality, smaller lot sizes, faster delivery, *and* lower cost. Traditional companies might have been able to offer the first three—but with *higher* cost. That is why traditional manufacturers have had to reinvent themselves in order to survive.

West Bend met the challenge and won. We will explore exactly what West Bend did and why it worked throughout this chapter. Getting there required dramatic changes in work design.

Hundreds of companies have faced the same challenge presented to West Bend. First, manufacturers have had to completely change traditional methods, introducing *lean manufacturing* in order to achieve the dramatic improvements in cost, quality, productivity, and customer service that wins market share. Although the events began in manufacturing, the challenge is just as real today for the service sector, including banking and finance, hospitality, health, retail, transportation, education, and other services.

What Is Work Design?

There are three elements to work design that are the foundation of any work system. They were referred to in Chapter 1 and include people, decisions, and information. At a practical level, these three components manifest themselves as physical and mental processes. For example, if I really want to know what an airplane pilot does, I must get to know the three components that make up the design of a pilot's work:

1. *People locus*—the actual tasks or activities the worker performs. In the pilot's case, some tasks are physical (manipulating controls, reading instruments), while others are mental (calculating weight ratios for takeoff speed). All work consists of activities.
2. *Decision locus*—the decisions required to accomplish the tasks and achieve desired results, such as selecting altitudes, approach speeds, and headings.
3. *Information locus*—the information the pilot must have in order to make the right decisions. This includes information from instruments, instructions from air traffic controllers and visual feedback.

Traditional Work Design

Much of the work design we see in organizations today is a product of thinking that dates back almost one hundred years to the principles of F. W. Taylor—a doctrine that has been labeled Scientific Management or Taylorism. His ideas can be summarized by the following rules:

1. Break down work into its simplest parts and have each worker do the same task over and over.
2. Structure work according to strict discipline.
3. Organize work according to functions.
4. Exercise strict supervision of workers to insure that they do what they are told and that they do not cheat.[2]

Henry Ford's assembly line is, perhaps, the most famous manifestation of Taylorism. The system still characterizes traditional work designs today. Figure 4.1 presents an illustration of such a system. The traditional work design illustrated here has three defining characteristics. First, command and control over the system is achieved by creating a series of functional hierarchies or chimneys of authority:

• *Authority over sales.* The sales organization "owns" the customer and is the only point of contact between the company and the customer. The sales rep takes orders and they are

Figure 4.1 Traditional Work Design

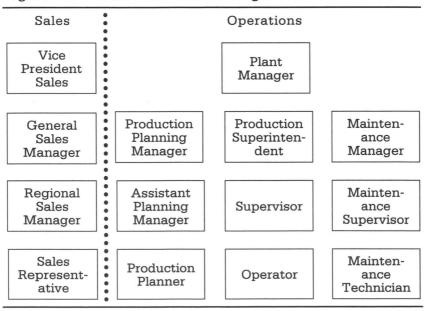

Sales		Operations		
Vice President Sales		Plant Manager		
General Sales Manager	Production Planning Manager	Production Superintendent	Maintenance Manager	
Regional Sales Manager	Assistant Planning Manager	Supervisor	Maintenance Supervisor	
Sales Representative	Production Planner	Operator	Maintenance Technician	

processed within the sales organization (to the left of the dotted line in the figure).

• *Authority over planning.* The planning organization (within Operations) "owns" the planning process. Taking orders handed off by the sales organization, workers in this organization plan and schedule production.

• *Authority over manufacture.* Workers in this organization actually produce the product. They "own" manufacture. Managers give instructions to supervisors who, in turn, tell workers what to do hour by hour. Workers, in turn, are organized into many sub-departments and narrow job classifications, each with its own description. An operator, for example, may perform only one task, in one area, over and over again. One operator at West Bend, for example, when asked, "What is your job?" responded, "I attach the handles to the pots."

• *Authority over maintenance.* Workers in this organization "own" the equipment. Workers in this department perform preventive maintenance, repair and overhaul equipment, set up the equipment, and perform product changeovers.

There are several levels of supervision necessary to get work done and the work itself entails many hand-offs between people and across functions.

The second characteristic of traditional work designs is well-defined spheres of activity, each with narrowly bounded areas of responsibility and accountability. The boxes in the system define very clearly "what is my job" and "what is not my job." Each box in Figure 4.1 represents a separate job classification. In fact, some of the boxes in the figure may include multiple job classifications.

The third characteristic of a traditional work design is division of labor. Technical work is compartmentalized into the jobs of a few experts, while the work of the majority is made as simple as possible. The result is that most workers can be treated as replaceable parts. The few experts have no incentive for sharing their knowledge with others—and giving up the power base that preserves their control over others.

Indeed, traditional work designs have one defining characteristic: they are an effective tool for management to exert control. In an age of global competition, high technology, and knowledge work, however, they have severe limitations. Companies can no longer afford to have workers who lack a fundamental understanding of how they contribute to key measures, as illustrated by the Score Card in Figure 4.2.

The greatest limitation of traditional work designs is that they are slow and inflexible. In our West Bend example, the process of customer fulfillment (beginning with retailers' needs and ending with on-time delivery of quality merchandise to their shelves) required numerous hand-offs within and between functional hierarchies. The result was that the process took too much time.

Second, traditional designs are expensive. Time is money. Traditional work designs require "buffers" of inventory in order to keep people busy. Thus, the work areas are choked with partially completed products waiting for the next step in the process or waiting to be repaired. Inventory costs money—the more of it a company has on any given day, the higher its cost of production.

Third, traditional work designs result in high levels of quality defects. Thus, more money is spent correcting defects and problems that are not caught before a final quality audit—or not caught at all until an angry customer returns a defective product to the store.

Finally, traditional work arrangements are oriented toward

Figure 4. 2 Traditional Work Design Score Card

Business Score Card	
Unit cost	Too high
Quality	Too low
Inventory	Too high
Delivery (cycle time)	Too long

occupational functions which are internally focused, rather than designed around core business, customer-focused processes. For example, sales are "owned" by the sales organization, but orders are fulfilled by the manufacturing organization. The result is that the very steps in the process that are most important to customers—and, therefore, most important to long-term business success—may fall through the cracks.

Traditional work arrangements are too slow, too costly, and distract everyone's attention from tending to core business processes, and ultimately, customer needs.

Virtual Work Design

In recent years, Intel Corporation has cut time to market with semiconductors dramatically. Sony Electronics achieves benchmark performance on continuous improvement by building Kaizen (continuous improvement) directly into its manufacturing processes. Automobile manufacturers in recent years have cut defect rates by several orders of magnitude. Insurance companies have achieved mass customization in creating unique financial products for customers in an instant, when traditional application processes used to take several weeks and offered few choices.

What's happened? What's different? Intel, Sony, and others have unleashed performance by totally redesigning work. Through a process of reinvention called lean manufacturing, the companies changed their work design from that illustrated in Figure 4.1 to that illustrated in Figure 4.3[A].

Figure 4.3[A] illustrates a high-performance work design supportive of a customer-focused business process. First, as you can see, the functional silos have disappeared. The virtual work design is triggered by a need (sales) and ends with fulfillment of that need (high-quality product delivered to the customer, on time, at low cost). The columns of the matrix represented in Figure 4.3[A] consist of steps in an entire process of customer fulfillment. Many of the activities that were segregated into specialist job classifications and functional silos are unbundled

(text continues on page 86)

Figure 4.3 Virtual Work Design

[A]

	Customer Fulfillment Business Processes							
	Core			Support				Team
	Sales	Customer Inventory	Product Planning	Materials Management	Assembly	Shipping	Quality	Maintenance	Team
Advanced-level skills									
Accomplished-level skills									
Entry-level skills									

[B]

Customer Fulfillment Business Processes

	Core					Support			Team
	Sales	Customer Inventory	Product Planning	Materials Management	Assembly	Shipping	Quality	Maintenance	Team
Advanced-level skills					▓				
Accomplished-level skills					▓				
Entry-level skills	▓	▓	▓	▓	▓	▓	▓	▓	▓

▓ Assembly Career Path

and invested in self-directed teams that "own" the entire work design represented by the matrix in Figure 4.3[A]. In a traditional design, nobody "owned" customer fulfillment. In fact, if one were to ask workers in a traditional work design who the customer is, the response from most would be, "I don't know!" or "My boss."

Second, work is structured much differently in a virtual work team. Individual team members do not have a "job" in the traditional sense. Rather, each member has a role defined by the depth and breadth of skills required to perform in a given process. The role consists of some combination of skills (frequently referred to as *skill blocks*) in the matrix defining the work design. These roles are often called *skill paths* or *career paths*. Each skill path involves both breadth and depth of skill. The skill paths overlap to a degree, yet roles can be somewhat specialized. Figure 4.3[B] outlines one career path for assembly which includes depth in its assembly skills and breadth in the whole process, providing for flexibility without sacrificing expertise.

Third, the work design matrix in Figure 4.3[A] involves three classes or types of work activities:

1. *The core business process*—sales, customer inventory, materials management, product planning, assembly
2. *Support processes*—shipping, quality and maintenance
3. *Team processes*—group decision-making, problem-solving, and self-management

Finally, teams now can be organized around the work design and its underlying business process. In the example illustrated in Figure 4.3, there might be twenty employees constituting a customer fulfillment team who jointly are accountable for the entire process. The team is jointly accountable for a single score card defining process excellence (represented in Figure 4.4).

Figure 4.4 Virtual Work Design Score Card

Business Score Card	
Unit cost	Low
Quality	World-class
Inventory	Minimal
Delivery	100% fill rate

Dramatic Change in Virtual Roles

Work is much different in a virtual work design. Managers, operators, and technical people find that their lives change dramatically in the shift from traditional to virtual work designs illustrated in Figure 4.5 on the next page.

The transition from traditional to virtual work designs can be difficult for all parties—managers, supervisors, operators, and technical personnel. The change requires stretching people beyond narrow, predictable jobs, often threatening shifts in assumptions about who does what and who is accountable for what. The changes summarized in Figure 4.5 are:

• Managers shift from attending to day-to-day issues toward managing the future. They must shift to a concentration on long-term vision and strategy for the operation. They remain responsible for ensuring that appropriate resources are in place, but their planning horizon lengthens.

• First-level supervisors are the individuals most impacted by the shift from a traditional to a virtual workplace, yet, ironically, they are most frequently ignored when the change takes place. Shifting to a virtual arrangement can take a severe toll on supervisors if they are ignored. Their success is no longer achieved by giving orders, but by delegating many decisions. They shift from being immediate, hourly supervisors of their employees, involved in daily decisions, to teaching, coaching, and supporting long-term skill development. They no longer operate from a traditional authority base.

Figure 4.5 Traditional vs. Virtual Work Design

Position	Traditional	Virtual
Manager	Oversees operations, assembles resources.	Establishes long-term vision, ensures resources.
First-level supervisor	Directly oversees work and manages employees. Gives orders, ensures they are followed, and makes all decisions about the work.	Role shifts from supervisor to leader. Delegates many decisions. Coaches and teaches rather than giving orders. Supports team processes.
Operators and administrative employees	Work as individual contributors, focus on single-skilled operational tasks.	Work as members of a self-directed team, carrying out a variety of activities including operations, technical support, process improvement, and management.
Technical specialists (e.g., mechanic, engineer, underwriter)	Operate as an individual contributors, defining and executing technical work in order to support operations.	Operate as advisers, teachers, and coaches for the team. Share technical expertise and teach team members how to conduct technical activities.

• Operators and administrative employees also face an enormous change in roles. In a traditional work environment, they operate as single-skilled, individual contributors. As members of a team, they share collective responsibility for an entire process, often guiding a product from raw materials to a customer's hands.

In addition to taking on a greater breadth and depth of operational activities, team members also must take on support and management activities once reserved for specialists, supervisors, and managers. As a result, the team becomes self-directed or self-managed. Team members, for example, perform preventive maintenance, assess quality, control processes, apply statistical process control, make inventory decisions, conduct product changeovers, schedule production, conduct meetings, and, in some cases, even make human resource decisions. At the extreme, the team is self-managed, needing no direct supervision.

• Finally, specialists are impacted by virtual work designs. In a traditional environment, technical people (engineers, accountants, mechanics, electricians, actuaries, underwriters, and others) have been accustomed to operating alone, as individual contributors, from a personal and occupational skill base. Underwriters, for example, work in an office making decisions on accepting policy applications. Similarly, tool and die makers work in a lab and come out to the line only to set up equipment for a product changeover. In a virtual workplace specialists face the counter-intuitive demand to teach and show others what they can do.

Teaching others to perform preventive maintenance or other specialized activities poses two threats to the specialist. First, skill dilution becomes an issue. The technician who has years of experience (and perhaps specialized training) may not want to share that expertise and status. Second, specialists may fear losing their jobs if they teach team members everything that they need to do. In reality, however, we have found that specialists usually have nothing to fear in the transition to the virtual workplace. Yet, their work does change in two directions. First, having others perform routine technical work frees the expert to concentrate on higher-order problems. Second, he or she can devote more time to specialized projects, focusing on continuous improvement. Intel, the semiconductor manufacturer, was an early creator of virtual workplaces and the use of self-directed teams. When the transition to virtual workplaces was made, the firm still needed technicians and engineers. Their roles changed dramatically, however, in order to leverage their expertise more rapidly across more people and greater production volume than encountered in a traditional setting.

Differences in Work Design Between Traditional and Virtual Workplaces

Figure 4.6 summarizes the differences between work designs in traditional and virtual workplaces. The three foundations of work design—people, decisions and information locus—change dramatically. However, all virtual workplaces are not the same. In fact, as we discussed in Chapter 3, there are three types of virtual workplaces. The description of West Bend represents the cyberlink workplace, with the greatest corresponding degree of change from the traditional workplace. Telecommuting and frontline workplaces present less dramatic departures.

   • *People locus.* In the traditional workplace, people focus on narrow tasks as individual contributors to the work being done. Work design in the virtual workplace ranges from individual contributor (telecommuting) to combined sales and service roles (frontline) to broad roles that combine many steps in a customer-focused work process (cyberlink).

   • *Decision locus.* Virtual workplaces are faster, and speed requires changes in decision making. In a traditional setting, decision making is highly controlled and hierarchical. Operational processes are standardized and "idiot-proofed." Exceptions must be handled by referral up through command and control

Figure 4.6 Traditional vs. Virtual Work Design

Work Design Element	Traditional Work Design	Virtual Work Design		
		Tele-commuting	Frontline	Cyberlink
People locus	Focus on a narrow set of tasks as an individual contributor	Inividual contributor	Combined sales and service role	Extensive breadth and depth of skills related to the business process
Decision locus	Manage the process through command and control hierarchies	Telecom-muters make more independent decisions than their traditional counterparts	Decisions made on the customer's premises	Natural work teams make "real-time" decisions
Information locus	Information restricted and available on a need-to-know basis only	"Real time" information available	"Real-time" information available	"Real-time" information available

hierarchies. In a virtual workplace, decision making is dispersed and empowered. In the interest of speed, virtual organizations drive decision making close to the customer. Telecommuters will make more independent decisions than their counterparts in traditional workplaces due to their physical isolation. The nature of the frontline role lends itself to joint decision making with the customer on the customer's premises. The cyberlink workplace is team-based, with a natural work team making real-time decisions.

• *Information locus.* Effective decisions also require timely and user-friendly information. In a traditional workplace, information is power. It is highly restricted and doled out only on a need-to-know basis.

A virtual workplace requires that information be available in real time to all. This is true for all three forms of the virtual workplace. West Bend provides a vivid example of the power of technology married to a cyberlink work system. The customer fulfillment process illustrated in Figure 4.1 required a series of hand-offs that required two weeks to work through. In addition, the company had to run big lot sizes and could not deliver "ones and twos" of any product on short notice. In order to meet Wal-Mart's demands and win its business, West Bend introduced technological change by introducing lean manufacturing methods and information technology. West Bend accomplished this by establishing online links between Wal-Mart's point of sale inventory systems and West Bend's production floor. The two companies created a virtual workplace—a seamless relationship between them. Today, West Bend production employees start each day by consulting terminals in their area that are tied into customer inventory systems. The result: West Bend employees can make hourly production schedule decisions that allow them to ship customers' orders within hours while minimizing work in process and finished goods inventories. West Bend has slashed costs, increased quality dramatically, and met all of its customers' needs. Such an outcome would have been impossible in a traditional workplace.

The virtual workplace has a dramatic and positive impact on employees as well. Engaging in virtual arrangements causes employees to extend *line of sight* (understanding of key business results and how their activities influence such outcomes) and *line of impact* (a sense of confidence that the individual and the team can impact bottom-line business results). The West Bend operator, for example, who once told us that her job was to "attach the handles to the pots," developed new insights into her work. After experiencing work in a design similar to that illustrated in Figure 4.3 and working under a group incentive system, she answered quite differently when asked what her job was three years later: "See those products over there?" she asked, pointing to a display table. "Those are one hundred forty SKUs that my team owns and we're the best in the business. We have halved the inventory levels we work with, taken significant cost out, have 100 percent quality, and were named vendor of the year by Wal-Mart, our biggest customer!" The operator's line of sight expanded from a single-task job to that of a business-person who knows her customer, knows her products, and knows how to achieve maximal customer and financial results.

Getting to Virtual Work Design

In order to adopt a virtual work design, an organization must go through three distinct steps:

1. *Restructure around processes rather than functions.* Adopt a customer-focused approach to operations that cuts through functional departments and silos.
2. *Develop a work design matrix.* Create a framework that does away with "jobs" and moves toward an array of skills associated with processes.
3. *Create career paths for team members.* Tie together the skills that represent the depth and breadth of the process.

Following is an overview of each step.

Restructuring Around Processes Rather Than Function

Traditional organizations tend to be structured around functions where similar types of work activities occur. For example, those individuals who participate in an organization that requires a look at or change to an organization's "books" must pass through the accounting department. Those individuals who participate in the design of a product form the engineering or research and development function; typically, nothing about a product ever changes without these folks involved. Human resource experts control hiring, training, compensation, and performance management. Production makes (or remakes) the product itself. Production control does the scheduling. Quality assurance exists to ensure that the product is good enough to sell. The sales division distributes products to customers. Customer service handles customer complaints, and so on.

Virtual organizations, by contrast, are structured around end-to-end, customer-driven processes. For example, a resort company assembles a team consisting of everyone who comes into contact with a guest during the arrival or departure process. Similarly, an aircraft manufacturer places all team members involved with the final stages of body frame configuration together. A customer-focused sales team consists of a product expert, a technician, a deal-maker, and a documentation expert. An appliance manufacturer uses groups of assemblers to take its product from skeleton to washing machine.

Developing a process-oriented structure begins by examining the organization through a process lens and identifying the customer-driven process that the company will perform. This means identifying the processes that create value for customers. A *process* can be defined as narrowly as "beginning to end sheet metal assembly," or as broadly as "lead generation through purchase and repeat business." Some companies consider all of their manufacturing efforts to be a process. Others consider manufacturing to be a single step in a much larger process. Some companies consider sales a process unto itself. Others consider sales the culmination of a larger effort. Defining business processes is an art rather than a science. In general, a business process is a set of activities with clear inputs and outputs that deliver value to customers.

Most companies define processes by having internal experts (usually the people who perform the work on a daily basis) conduct process mapping sessions with the help of facilitators. They start by agreeing on process scope: what event triggers the process (the "trigger" event) and what event concludes the process (the "concluding" event). Next, they go chronologically through the process from the perspective of the customer, identifying each step along the way. These occurrences may consist of *inputs* (material or information being added to the process), *activities* (employees conducting work), *outputs* (product, material, or information being removed from the process) and *customer touch points* (points of customer interaction). Finally, the group agrees on the event that concludes the process.

When the process mapping sessions are complete, teams are defined around end-to-end processes based on logical team composition factors such as size, geographic proximity, similarity of skills, and interdependence of work. Once a team has been defined, it then arranges the steps into logical process categories or groupings based on the natural breaks in the process. These categories represent "chunks" of the whole process that individuals progress through in a skill progression. These groupings will form the columns of a work system matrix (described in the next section). The work system matrix represents the work of a team defined around end-to-end processes whose ultimate results require the completion of all steps along the process.

Defining the Work in the Process as a Matrix

In a virtual organization, the organization chart is replaced by a *work system matrix*. The work system matrix is a device that marries the process categories or groupings defined in the previous step (columns) and consistent levels of complexity (rows). Let's say, for example, that we have defined a process whose trigger is a guest making a decision to book a room at a resort and whose concluding event is the guest leaving the resort at the end of her stay. Based on our process mapping, we might have the following process categories:

- Reservation/guest service
- Arrival
- Recreation
- Food and beverage
- Merchandise
- Upkeep and maintenance
- Team support

These process categories would translate into vertical columns on a matrix that looks something like Figure 4.7.

The horizontal rows indicate the level of skills within each column. Generally, entry-level skills are consistent with basic understanding and/or operation of procedures or services (e.g., operate keyboard, empty trash, greet guest). Accomplished-level skills require some training or experience, and are consistent with complex, non-routine and/or troubleshooting procedures or services (e.g., correct reservation data, inspect room, identify guest need). Advanced-level skills require significant training or experience, and are consistent with improving upon and/or inventing new procedures or services (e.g., correct billing dispute, develop new housekeeping process, address complex guest relations issue). Generally, advanced-level activities are consistent with those activities performed by frontline team leaders, supervisors, or managers.

Creating Career Paths Defining Depth and Breadth

In virtual organizations, jobs are replaced by career path roles. In traditional organizations, responsibilities are delineated by titles such as accountant, punch press operator, front desk clerk, telephone operator, production supervisor, or quality inspector. Each title describes a job with specific responsibilities.

Figure 4.7 Resort Work Design Matrix

	Reservation/ Guest Service	Arrival	Recreation	Food & Beverage	Merchandise	Upkeep and Maintenance	Team Support
Advanced							
Accomplished							
Entry							

Career paths in a work system matrix accomplish the same goal, but do so in a much more fluid way. Each career path role comprises a set of skill blocks from the work system matrix. In general, each career path represents both depth (vertical blocks) and breadth (horizontal blocks). By containing overlapping career paths, virtual organizations are flexible and dynamic. For employees, this offers career opportunities well beyond traditional roles that are confined to narrow tasks.

Most virtual companies set up career paths that contain *core* blocks (those blocks required by all members of a given team) as well as *specialty* blocks for a given process category. This ensures an appropriate balance between having narrow specialists at one extreme and "jacks of all trades" at the other extreme.

Over the last five years, a number of leading companies have begun the transition toward the virtual workplace. We can benefit from their experience in contemplating what a virtual workplace would look like in our organizations and how to get there most effectively.

In the next section we will present and analyze the experience of two companies representing quite different industries and circumstances. The first case study involves moving to a frontline work system from a traditional sales organization. The second is a greenfield start-up of a hotel and recreation organization.

Case 1: ABC Corp.—Redefining Sales and Service To Meet Customer Needs

Business Situation: A Wake-Up Call From the Customers

This organization supplies plastic containers (for example, bottles, jugs, and related containers) to the beverage industry. Prior to the 1990s, ABC Corp. enjoyed a favorable position in the marketplace. In the early 1990s competition did develop in the market, both from other vendors and from potentially new technologies.

A first step in meeting competitive pressure was to visit with customers and ask, "How are we doing?" The answers were sobering. The company's biggest customer responded that, given a choice, it would do business with another company in an instant. ABC Corp. heard the following from its customers:

"You're hard to get hold of."
"Your delivery performance is subpar."
"I never know whom I'm dealing with in your organization."
"There are too many hand-offs in dealing with you."
"You're too expensive."

ABC recognized it was in a vulnerable position and responded by completely restructuring its business processes around the customer. Its restructuring called for drastic change in work design.

Frontline Work Design Strategy—The Business Case

The first step in getting to a virtual work design is to establish a vision for the system and establish metrics. ABC's vision included the following elements:

- Create customer fulfillment teams that have the breadth of skills to maximize customer fulfillment and customer satisfaction.
- Streamline the sales and service process.
- Eliminate functional silos.
- Create shared sales and service ownership within customer fulfillment teams.
- Reduce hand-offs—fix the problem on the first call.
- Get as many people into the field as possible.

ABC next created an Enterprise Report Card (ERC) and set goals on the following metrics:

- Time to market (defined as the time elapsed from new design creation to customer use)
- Cycle time (defined as the time elapsed in filling a customer order or resolving a customer issue)
- Unit cost (total cost per thousand units)
- Quality (parts per million defects leaving the company)
- Customer fulfillment (percentage of the time customers have received what they want, where they want it, how they want it)

Mapping the Old Business Process

The first step in reinventing ABC's business was to map its current business process. Figure 4.8 represents the business process that needed attention. A design team mapped and analyzed the current process and found the following faults:

- Too many departments (marketing, design, production, and sales) working at odds with each other
- Too many hand-offs in the process between product design and customer fulfillment
- Multiple points of contact for the customer
- Too many dropped batons, resulting in inconsistent service
- Intramural rivalry between departments
- Unacceptably high rates of defects found by the customer

The resulting report card was unacceptable. Too much time to market, too high a cost, and low levels of quality, resulting in dangerous levels of customer dissatisfaction.

Restructure the Business Process With a Virtual Organization

ABC restructured or reinvented its business process to survive and prosper in a new marketplace. The answer

Figure 4.8 Traditional Product Design and Sales Process

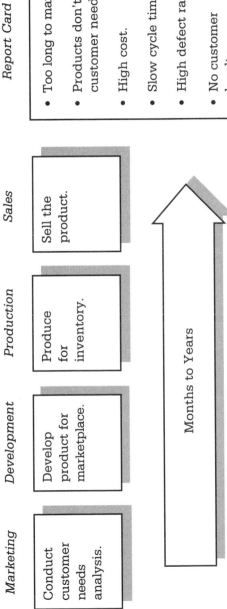

Marketing	Design and Development	Production	Sales
Conduct customer needs analysis.	Develop product for marketplace.	Produce for inventory.	Sell the product.

Months to Years

Report Card

- Too long to market.
- Products don't fit customer needs.
- High cost.
- Slow cycle time.
- High defect rates.
- No customer loyalty.

was to become a virtual organization with its customer (and suppliers). A virtual organization requires that boundaries between and within organizations disappear to be replaced by a seamless process, in this case, that begins with customer needs and ends with customer fulfillment.

A virtual organization requires a virtual business process—joining ABC with its customers. The process invented at ABC is illustrated in Figure 4.9. Note that both ABC and the customer are part of the same process. The process begins with the customer's needs: for containers with given characteristics, delivered to satisfy just-in-time inventory requirements, at minimum cost, and 100 percent quality.

A Virtual Organization Requires a Virtual Workplace

ABC required a transition from a traditional work design to a virtual work design. The old organization was characterized by separate departments with over forty different job classifications. The new organization had one single integrated team that owned the entire process illustrated in Figure 4.9. The process maps emerging from the redesign became the basis for establishing the work design illustrated in Figure 4.10. The several departments and multiple job classifications are replaced by a single team focused on a customer. The team owns the relationship with the customer and has all the skills to manage an entire process of customer fulfillment. The workforce strategy is to build processes around the customer and build teams around the process. The customer team covered diverse technical skill sets and team skills to support the capabilities of the team members. The team was also accountable for maximizing metrics associated with the process on the Enterprise Report Card:

Figure 4.9 Virtual Customer Fulfillment Process

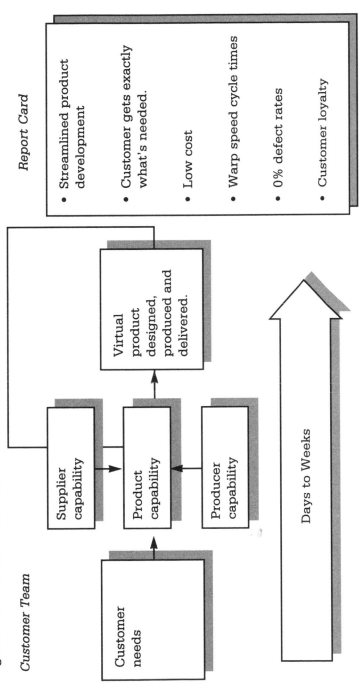

Report Card

- Streamlined product development
- Customer gets exactly what's needed.
- Low cost
- Warp speed cycle times
- 0% defect rates
- Customer loyalty

Customer Team

Customer needs

Supplier capability

Product capability

Producer capability

Virtual product designed, produced and delivered.

Days to Weeks

Figure 4.10 Customer Team Work Matrix

	Selling	Development	Manufacturing	Delivery	Team
Marketing					
Advanced					
Accomplished					
Entry					

- *Time to market*—the time elapsed from new design creation to customer use
- *Cycle time*—the time elapsed in filling a customer order or resolving a customer issue
- *Unit cost*—total cost per thousand units
- *Quality*—parts per million defects leaving the company
- *Customer fulfillment*—percentage of the time the customers have received what they want, where they want it, how they want it

As the teams became more sophisticated in their business process, they got to know their customers more intimately. They learned through contact with customers, for example, that the greatest factor that upsets a customer is bringing on product that varies so much in a specific dimension that it throws off the customer's container-filling process, resulting in expensive downtime and repair. Responding to that issue, the team developed methods that would maximize processibility—that is, the degree to which products run smoothly in the customer's process.

Defining Roles According to Key Processes

ABC defined roles on the customer team according to overlapping skill paths. ABC's system is illustrated in Figure 4.11. The skill path illustrated consists of core blocks (those competencies all team members must have) and specialty blocks (those that are unique to each role). In this case ABC identified six basic roles on the team, corresponding to each of the process steps in Figure 4.11. What makes these roles different from traditional job classifications is that they overlap in terms of core and (in some cases) specialty blocks. The result is that the team functions as a unit with minimal handoffs. Team skills (the fifth column) relate to skills that are required if a team is to function well. All members of

Figure 4.11 Skill Paths on the Customer Team

Marketing	Selling	Development	Manufacturing	Delivery	Team
Advanced					
Accomplished					
Entry					

Core Block

Specialty Block

the team must possess entry-level skills related to communication, human relations, and team management processes. Some members of the team will specialize in team functioning and therefore will possess higher-level team skills. The skill path requires both depth and breadth that go well beyond the confines of a traditional job classification.

What Has ABC Gained?

ABC faced a crisis: how to dramatically improve customer performance as competition developed in a market where it once operated under monopoly conditions. Organizational restructuring was only the first step to achieving competitive advantage. Landing the vision and executing the restructuring effort required radical transformation of work design, as well as pay (a topic we will cover in Chapter 6).

What has ABC gained from the new work design? Subsequent review of ABC's experience suggests the following:

For ABC

- Quicker cycle time (time from initial order to customer delivery)
- Greater customer intimacy
- Minimal hand-offs
- One point of contact for the customer
- Improved customer satisfaction

For Employees

- Increased earning opportunity
- More interesting work
- Greater intimacy with the customer
- Greater sense of control over the business
- Greater sense of job security

Case 2: California Beach Resort

Business Situation: Resort Growth

A major hospitality and leisure company achieved unparalleled success in creating vacation memories at resort destinations around the world. Each property involves recreation and entertainment combined with resort facilities. The Company was expanding its product offering to include lower-cost, stand-alone resorts in several key vacation destinations throughout North America.

The major strategic challenge faced by the Company was to achieve success without the surrounding structures and processes of an integrated property. Specifically, the Company faced the following concerns:

- Provide the highest level of guest experience at the lowest cost to resort customers.
- Transport the big resort culture and values without transporting the big resort structure.
- Maximize the efficiency of operations by eliminating workforce downtime created by guest activity patterns (check-in/check-out, sleeping, dining, sports, activities).

Cyberlink Work Design Strategy—The Business Case

The Company's vision included the following elements:

- Achieve unsurpassed levels of guest service.
- Have fewer employees, doing more, earning more, and happier.
- Have the experts where they are needed based on guest patterns.

The Company is extraordinarily effective in understanding and measuring customer service. Figure 4.12 illustrates the model employed to make business decisions and to measure the effectiveness of a resort property. Three levels of measurement are involved. Ultimately, the Company seeks to maximize the bottom line. Accomplishing the goal requires customer loyalty (return visits), market share, and revenue. Such bottom-line measures can be achieved in the long term only by maximizing resort operations. The Company keeps careful track of operations metrics such as occupancy rate, cost per room night, and customer satisfaction. At the work design level, the Company knows what drives operational results. These are called *contact measures*, those things the Company can influence on a daily basis that drive operations and resort performance. They include such metrics as number of staff carrying bags, percentage of orders correct, guest waiting times, resort cleanliness, and material waste.

The Resort Process

The first step was to restructure the business process. Figure 4.13 illustrates the work design matrix for resort operations. Note that the work design captures processes that cut across the traditional boundaries between the front of the house and the back of the house. Arrival represents the process of greeting arriving guests and getting them settled. The process includes front desk and concierge operations. Upkeep refers to all housekeeping activities. Engineering refers to maintenance processes. Recreation refers to all operations involving organized guest activities, including sports. Food and beverage (F&B) includes restaurant and lounge operations. Merchandise refers to gift shop operations. Finally, the staff is considered a team and is responsible for team activities. The team is also accountable for maximizing metrics associated with the process, in this case:

Figure 4.12 Beach Resort Measurements

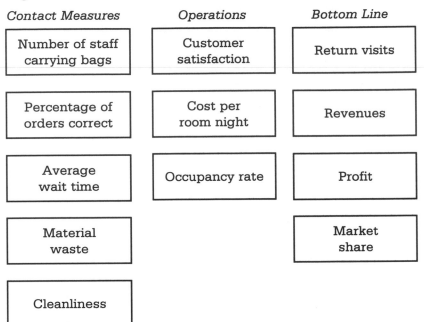

Contact Measures   *Operations*   *Bottom Line*

Number of staff carrying bags	Customer satisfaction	Return visits

| Percentage of orders correct | Cost per room night | Revenues |

| Average wait time | Occupancy rate | Profit |

| Material waste | | Market share |

| Cleanliness | | |

- *Number of staff carrying bags*—measured as the percentage of staff assisting with luggage during peak check-in/check-out times
- *Average guest waiting time*—defined as the time a guest waits to check in, get a restaurant table, or use recreational facilities during peak use periods
- *Cost per guest night*—defined as the total cost—labor, overhead, materials—per room night
- *Cleanliness*—defined as property appearance, including trash, edging, and sweeping
- *Customer satisfaction*—defined as summary statistics of actual guest ratings compared to statistical norms in guest satisfaction surveys

The second step was to develop career paths that created specific sets of skills for each member of the team.

Figure 4.13 Beach Resort Work Design Matrix

	Arrival	Upkeep	Engineering	Recreation	F&B	Merchandise	Team
Advanced							
Accomplished							
Entry							

Figure 4.14 displays one career path with core blocks representing breadth and specialty blocks representing higher levels of skills in the specialty areas.

What Has the Company Gained?

A review of the resort's experience suggests the following:

For the Company

- Reduced unit cost (cost per room night)
- Greater guest intimacy
- Minimum guest hand-offs
- Increased profit margins

For Employees

- Increased earning opportunity
- More interesting work
- Greater intimacy with guests
- Greater sense of value
- Greater employability

Virtual Work Designs: What We Have Learned

The most intriguing—and perhaps exciting—learning from our experience in helping companies transition from traditional to virtual work designs is that the virtual workplace is both customer- and employee-friendly. As we discussed in our West Bend example, Wal-Mart was able to make demands regarding cycle time, quality, and product cost that simply would have been unheard of in a traditional work environment. No traditional supplier—regardless of its intent—could have delivered on Wal-Mart's demands and remained financially solvent. As far as employees are concerned, contrasting public sentiment regarding the evils of re-engineering (e.g., layoffs, downsizing, lack of employment security), we have found that companies using virtual

Figure 4.14 Skill Paths on the Customer Team

	Arrival	Upkeep	Engineering	Recreation	F&B	Merchandise	Team
Advanced	Specialty Block						
Accomplished	Specialty Block			Specialty Block		Specialty Block	Core Block
Entry	Core Block	Core Block	Core Block	Core Block	Core Block	Core Block	Core Block

Specialty Block

Core Block

work designs have been able to offer employees unparalleled opportunities in terms of learning and earning potential. In all of our cited examples, employees operating in virtual work designs receive more training, perform broader and more interesting work on a daily basis, become closer to customers, maintain a greater sense of value, and have greater upside earning opportunity. All of these benefits lead to greater employability and long-term employment security. Elated customers and satisfied employees help lead these companies to long-term operational and financial success, allowing for a "win-win-win" outcome. Only by shattering traditional notions about hierarchy and control can companies unleash their potential in the new virtual workplace.

Notes

1. Adapted from Marc J. Wallace, Jr., and N. Fredric Crandall, "Winning In the Age of Execution: The Central Role of Work-Force Effectiveness," *American Compensation Association Journal*. Winter 1992/93.
2. F.W. Taylor, "Principles of Scientific Management," New York: Harper, 1991.

5

Skills and Competencies

In the virtual workplace, what people do is centered around an ongoing process. The dynamics of the process are driven by an organization that is far beyond the control of an individual worker and his or her own work. Things don't start and stop when we want them to. When I leave the office at 6:00 P.M. on Tuesday, work that I was doing may be "pulled up" on someone else's computer, and by the time I get back on Wednesday morning it may have changed dramatically. It is no longer *my* work and work isn't centered around *me*.

Many different types of skills and capabilities are required in this workplace. It is clear that a worker must be flexible in this environment. One must be willing and capable of doing the variety of tasks demanded by a complete process when it is required. One must also become disciplined to work independently or with small teams with a minimum of supervision. Face-to-face meetings may take place infrequently, and a substantial amount of communication may take place by e-mail, fax, and teleconference. In addition, there is a much broader set of knowledge required. While this will differ by the type of work done, the key is the need for breadth and depth across traditional occupations. For example, on the manufacturing floor, narrow job descriptions give way to broad "roles" on teams that encompass many steps in the production process. Traditional occupational barriers are broken, placing assembly work alongside maintenance work. Similarly, professional occupations such as engineering expand to include customer-related functions in sales and servicing.

In this chapter, we will first explore the roles of skills and competencies in the virtual workplace. We will then investigate who will be responsible for skill development. We will then review the role of teams and how they develop. Finally, we will introduce a new model for the career in the virtual workplace.

Skills and Competencies in the Virtual Workplace

Whenever we bring up the subject of skills and competencies, confusion arises over the definition of the terms. Skills and competencies in the virtual workplace may reflect on the organization and its *strategic* requirements to achieve competitive advantage (e.g., innovation, technology, customer responsiveness). Or, the subject may refer to *process* competencies, reflecting the skill and knowledge defined by a customer-driven process. Or, the subject may refer to *individual* competencies, the characteristics that underlie an individual's or team's capability to be effective in the virtual workplace.

What Is the Most Important Type of Competency in the Virtual Workplace?

In fact, all three types of competencies are required. Strategic competencies (see Figure 5.1) are core competencies of the organization that contribute to competitive advantage. They are "core" because they represent the basis for creating value for the organization. For example, product innovation is core for 3M Corporation. Consistency is core for McDonald's. High-quality

Figure 5.1 Strategic Competencies

Definition:	Core competencies of the organization that reflect an organization's collective learning and create competitive advantage
Examples:	Engineering (Honda Motor Co.) Innovation (3M) Product speed (FedEx) Consistency (McDonald's) Service (Ritz Carlton Hotels)
Underpinnings:	Business strategy; management science

service is core for Ritz Carlton Hotels. Without developing and utilizing these competencies, a company would be unsuccessful in pursuing its strategy and creating its own future.

Process competencies are driven by the business process itself. Because the virtual workplace is based on a fully integrated business process, it spans departmental and organizational boundaries. Therefore, the competency platform is based on the knowledge, activities, and performance results required of the whole process (see Figure 5.2). There are three types of process competencies:

1. *Operational (core) skills*—basic skills related to the process. For example, in manufacturing, these would include skills such as assembly, setup and machining. In a sales and service call center, they might include operating of telecommunication equipment, updating customer data, and responding to customer needs.

2. *Support skills*—skills supporting the operational process that previously could have resided in another department, such as engineering, maintenance, or administration.

3. *Interpersonal team skills*—include the skills required to effectively work in a collaborative multiskilling environ-

Figure 5.2 Process Competencies

Definition:	Effective process performance as defined by the knowledge required to perform process activities, the performance of the activities themselves, and the achievement of required skills
Examples:	Operational skills (assembly, machining, responding to customers) Support skills (administration, maintenance, information technology) Interpersonal team skills (problem solving, coaching, training)
Underpinnings:	Business process design theory; sociotechnical systems theory

ment. They include the basic capability of performing in a team environment through skills of collaboration, problem-solving, conflict resolution, coaching, and leadership.

Individual competencies are the underlying characteristics of people. As outlined in Figure 5.3, they include such skills as flexibility, cognitive skills, and a high achievement orientation. These skills are often utilized as a basis for selection in a battery of tests and structured interviews. Thus, they are generally considered predictors of job performance in a virtual workplace.

A virtual workplace requires all three of these competencies in order to be competitive and to get work done. Figure 5.4 shows the major differences between the three types of competencies. Individual competencies define who we are; process competencies describe what we do; and strategic competencies define what sets us apart from the rest.

Confusion around the meaning of competencies arises when we attempt to define work processes around strategic or individual competencies. Alternatively, there are problems when

Figure 5.3 Individual Competencies

Definition:	Underlying characteristics of an individual or team that can be shown to predict effective or superior performance.
Examples:	Flexibility Initiative Teamwork/cooperation High achievement orientation Advanced psychomotor skills Cognitive skills Interpersonal understanding
Underpinnings:	Industrial/organizational psychology; motivation theory.

Figure 5.4 Role of Skills and Competencies in the Virtual Workplace

Type of Competency	Definition	Role in the Virtual Workplace
Strategic	What separates us from the rest	Sets direction
Process	What we do	Describes work to be done
Individual	Who we are	Provides the basis for selection

we attempt to evaluate individual or team performance using strategic competencies as criteria and standards. Understanding and defining these different types of skills and competencies is extremely important in the virtual workplace because work encompasses process elements that stretch beyond traditional job classifications.

Process Skills and Work Design

Process skills are the underpinnings of work design. They provide a framework to get work done through actual activities. In the virtual workplace the three types of process skills—core, support, and team—comprise the breadth and depth of the work to be performed. Figure 5.5 summarizes the types of process skills required for telecommuting, frontline, and cyberlink workplaces.

Each successive model of the virtual workplace requires some unique skills and competencies. The telecommuting model, frontline model, and cyberlink model are serially additive, so that skills and competencies in the cyberlink model include those required in the first two. This is because each successive stage of the virtual workplace requires a greater degree of navigation and immersion.

Telecommuting Skills

Telecommuting involves one working in a remote location (most often the home) and establishing effective lines back to the "home base" organization and people on common work teams who may also be working remotely. The technical work that one does changes minimally. The special capabilities required involve the knowledge and skill to work independently and communicate effectively.

Support skills require information technology such as networking in with computer systems and frequent transfer of voice and data across systems. Time management and self-scheduling are important to telecommuting, especially when one may be in a position with family members closer to the work site than in a traditional work setting.

Frontline Skills

The frontline model combines customer sales and service related skills on the customer site. It often involves co-location of

Figure 5.5 Process Skills for Telecommuting, Frontline, and Cyberlink Workplaces

Process Steps	Work Design		
	Telecommuting	*Frontline*	*Cyberlink*
Operational skills	• Similar to traditional job	• Breadth of specialized technical skills across traditional jobs	• Breadth of specialized technical skills across traditional jobs
Support skills	• Information technology • Communications equipment	• Information technology • Communications equipment	• Technical skills for "support" areas such as administration, engineering, and maintenance included in natural work teams
Interpersonal and team skills	• Time management • Self-scheduling and work planning	• Adaptation to the social system of base and host companies	• Extensive skills and competencies for working in natural work teams crossing traditional boundaries

the services of many companies on a common site. These types of roles take many forms. For example, Allied Signal will co-locate its avionics inventory and staff on site at a Cessna facility to provide avionics equipment and support directly to the assembly line. In this case, there is specialized knowledge and skill required about the customer's products as well. Alternatively, companies in the business of selling, distributing, and servicing equipment in the field deploy sales and service teams to diverse geographic locations. The team members are home-based regionally, but work primarily on site on an on-demand basis when required. The sales and service team members need a broad set of technical skills as well as the flexibility and discipline to move around on a frequent basis.

The frontline skills focus on combining sales and service, which, in many companies, are separate occupations totally unconnected within the company. The reason that companies are combining sales and service in the field is to increase the effectiveness of the work process. This means that people placed in the process will be expected to adapt their world of work. It means that salespeople must learn service skills and service technicians need to understand and participate in the sales process. At the Cessna assembly facility, it means that Allied Signal employees become a part of the Cessna work system.

Representatives co-located in the field must be effectively tied back into their own organization. This requires the use of networked remote computers and work stations to receive the latest updates of sales and service information electronically.

Cyberlink Skills

The cyberlink model requires the most sophisticated skills because people are required to work collaboratively over the whole value chain, combining skills of the telecommuting and frontline models, but stretching them much further. There is extensive use of natural work teams that may be linked electronically rather than face-to-face. The natural work teams combine a much wider scope of skills, including many key processes of the organization. Finally, there may be extensive use of teams and individual contributors from many companies in the value chains that deliver their products and services to customers.

Flexibility and discipline take on a new meaning in the cyberlink organization. People devoted to managing a process must be prepared to make decisions on the spot and then communicate them quickly to all involved in order to keep the process up and going. At Intel, microprocessor manufacturing facilities (called FABS) teams work together on each shift to produce PC chips. Speed and quality are enhanced by the capability of team members to solve production problems on the line without stopping the production process. Members do this by working collaboratively even though they are all wearing "clean suits." In addition, information about production problems and their solutions are transferred from shift to shift. Managing in this fashion requires a dedication to the process that goes far beyond the real time of each individual involved—it requires a dedication to the process even at the times team members are not on shift.

The skill sets for people who work in the cyberlink environment are broad and deep. First, there is an extensive use of teams, as we have noted. The skills required to operate in a natural team environment include social and human resource competencies ranging from group dynamics to analytical problem solving. Of course, these social skills are enablers for the flexibility and discipline required of those who work in the process. Second, greater depth in technical skills is required if the members of the cyberlink organization are to be empowered to keep the process going on an indefinite basis. For example, machine operators must learn how to provide maintenance and repair for the equipment they operate. Likewise, engineers must be able to diagnose production problems and enable the solution on a real-time basis. Finally, all members of the process must be cross-trained in a very diverse set of skills that is usually supplemented by advanced information technology. For example, assemblers must be adept in product testing, quality control, and even shipping and receiving. Similarly, engineers must be capable of participating in sales/marketing and customer relations.

The Skill Block: Basic Building Block of the Virtual Workplace

In Chapter 3 we introduced the work design skill matrix. It arranges skill blocks by key process categories (operational, support, and team) in order to maximize productivity, quality, and customer satisfaction. The matrix is generally divided into three levels across each process category (entry, accomplished, and advanced) in order to distinguish the level of complexity or sophistication in performing an activity or a set of activities. Figure 5.6 outlines a sample skill block matrix for a sales process.

The matrix represents all of the work performed in a sales process. Operational skills include customer service, special customer problems, billing disputes, customer retention, and making sales offers. In a traditional workplace, each of these skills would most probably reside in a separate department. Sales support skills include administrative support, and team skills include the types of skills associated with working in and managing a natural work team environment. Each skill block includes detailed information in three areas specified in Figure 5.6: knowledge, activities and results:

1. *Knowledge*—the background information that is necessary to successfully complete the work. Knowledge can be gained through on-the-job or instructional training, structured self-instruction, or experience.

2. *Activities*—the work itself. Activities, generally found in a traditional job description, describe the work steps accomplished in the performance of duties.

3. *Results*—validation of acceptable performance. The results should be based as much as possible on quantifiable and objective work standards such as timeliness, quality, cost, service, and efficiency.

The information included in this skill block should be collected by a standard work analysis technique. It is usually developed when the work process is designed (see Chapter 4).

Figure 5.6 Sample Skill Matrix for the Sales Process

| | Operational | | | | | Support | |
	Customer Services	Handling Special Problems	Handling Billing Disputes	Customer Retention	Making Sales Offers	Sales Support	Team
Advanced							
Accomplished							
Entry	■						

Entry—Customer Service Skill Block

Knowledge

1. Knowledge of call flow and routing procedures
2. Ability to operate telephone console and headset
3. General knowledge of credit and credit card industry
4. Basic knowledge of credit process
5. Basic listening and problem-solving skills

Activity

1. Operate telephone console and headset; transfer calls as required
2. Explain key features of products and services
3. Respond to caller questions; provide solutions
4. Explain interest rate and billing principles

Results

1. Customer needs are met
2. Handling time is below 55 seconds/call
3. Aux time is below 12 minutes/call
4. 96% customer approval rating
5. 15% or lower callbacks

What About Team Skills?

The movement to teams has been a hallmark of high-performance organizations. As we have noted, teams are critical in the virtual workplace as well; however, there they play a very different role. In the high-performance organization, the team is a critical, if not the central vehicle for change, centering on intact natural work teams relying on frequent interpersonal relationships and interactions. In the virtual workplace, teaming and team behaviors play alongside information technology to deliver results. Indeed, "virtual teams," defined as groups of people working together through time and space, are fast becoming a regular part of our business vocabulary.

The way technology and teams work together is slightly different at each successive stage of the virtual workplace.

Telecommuting and Teams

In the telecommuting model, individuals work off site in isolation for long stretches of time, but they must maintain a team mindset because of the interdependencies that exist. It is necessary to do one's own work off site and make sure that it is in coordination, anticipating what others on the team will do. E-mail, faxing, and teleconferencing are aids to simulate an intact working situation.

Frontline and Teams

The frontline employee is the embodiment of the virtual team member. Networked information is crucial to get work done in the field. For example, the sales and service representative must ensure that he or she has the latest repair protocols; conversely, he or she must report innovative solutions to coworkers immediately so that other customers are served.

Cyberlink and Teams

The cyberlink workplace embodies a web of intact and virtual teams. For example, the West Bend Beverage Maker facility operates with intact cellular manufacturing teams on the production floor that receive just-in-time orders daily from business partner Wal-mart's customer order center. The intact teams coordinate production activities with the buying patterns of the worldwide network of Wal-mart customers in order to have daily turnaround of orders to fill shelves with the specific product configuration, where and when it is needed.

Developing Team Skills

The team skills that are needed in the virtual workplace are outlined in Figure 5.7. They include a comprehensive set of social skills with a foundation in effective interpersonal communication and interaction.

As Figure 5.7 shows, the team skills building blocks are the social skills that we normally associate with intact team development. They include the basic team skill of communication as a central theme, supported by the skills associated with social relationships (decision making, process analysis, conflict management) and the development of the team (planning and evaluation, problem solving, performance management, continuous learning, and team health). Each block in Figure 5.7 is broken down in more detail to provide insight into the specific types of team skills to be developed. It becomes clear that the required team-related skills are broad and deep.

However, team skills are not developed overnight. In fact, companies that have restructured around teams have found the transition usually takes up to five years to reach a steady state. Even when companies begin a team-based organization in a greenfield facility or business unit, there is a transformation process that takes a number of years.

Teams do not happen by accident, nor are they formed

Figure 5.7 Team Skills for the Virtual Workplace

Team Skills Building Blocks

Planning and Evaluation	Problem Solving	Decision Making
Team Health	Communication	Process Analysis
Continuous Learning	Conflict Management	Performance Management

Decision Making
• Team leader role
• Group decision making
• Consensus building
• Process improvement
• Accountability
• Influence

Process Analysis
• Process definition
• Process mapping
• Process improvement
• Process innovation
• SPC techniques
• Roles and responsibilities

Performance Management
• Goal-setting
• Objectives
• Performance tracking
• Coaching feedback
• Performance reviews
• Development planning

Conflict Management
• Conflict identification
• Resolution building
• Negotiation
• Consensus
• Compromising
• Resolution analysis

Communication
• Speaking
• Writing
• Listening
• Persuasion
• Meeting facilitation
• Asking questions

Problem Solving
• Data collection
• Analysis
• Options
• Solution development

Planning and Evaluation
• Priority setting
• Action planning
• Scheduling
• Accountability
• Quality of work/results evaluation

Team Health
• Trust development
• Commitment
• Group dynamics
• Interpersonal relations
• Involvement/ ownership

Continuous Learning
• Needs assessment
• On-the-job training
• Cross-training
• Coaching and mentoring
• Personal development
• Career planning

overnight. Team development should be planned systematically. A typical approach is outlined in Figure 5.8. It includes three steps in a process that takes at least sixty months. The first step is participative. It begins with basic cross-training in which team members concentrate on learning and performing each others' jobs. This initial step enhances the team's capability to work together and builds trust. Companies that have begun initially with training for higher team skills rather than with technical skills have developed teams capable of teamwork *without* the ability to perform technical skills as a team. Ultimately, this can lead to a team unable to advance from a participating to a self-sustaining level.

Self-sustaining teams begin to take on the capabilities of team maintenance. They do this in two ways. First, the team develops capability in support skills such as maintenance of equipment and administration. Support skills may also include activities such as basic engineering and drafting and financial management. These skills enable a substantial amount of autonomy or self-regulation. In addition, the team takes on social skills involving scheduling and planning, conducting its own meetings, and initial self-supervision.

The third step, self-management, is a level very few natural work teams ever achieve. It is an environment in which the team totally supports itself from a technical and social perspective. Activities include leadership and decision making as well as coordination with other teams. The reason why few natural teams reach this level fall into two areas. First, the time, effort and amount of training to achieve this level are costly. Many companies develop a vision for team development that stops at step 2, and determine that having self-sustaining teams is the ultimate step for the company. Alternatively, the actual experience of many companies that set off to reach step 3 of team development results in falling short of the goal. There may be a misunderstanding of the time and resources required, or the actual capability of company employees may fall short of reaching step 3 in the process.

Figure 5.8 Progression of Team Skills

Step 1: Participative	Step 2: Self-Sustaining	Step 3: Self-Managed	
Emphasize cross-training with a focus on technical skills	Team participates in support skills, planning, and self-supervision	Team totally supports itself, regulating and coordinating its own activities	
1–18 months	19–36 months	37–60+ months	

A New Model for a Career in the Virtual Workplace

Careers in the virtual workplace can take three diverse directions, as outlined in Figure 5.9. A traditional career path involves movement through promotions from job to job, usually based on some combination of time and service and/or merit. A traditional career does not really fit within the structure of the virtual workplace because it relies on promotions within a job hierarchy. This presents two problems. First, traditional promotions are made when job opportunities become open. A job opening implies that work does not necessarily stay with a team member; rather, the job stays

Figure 5.9 Careers in the Virtual Workplace

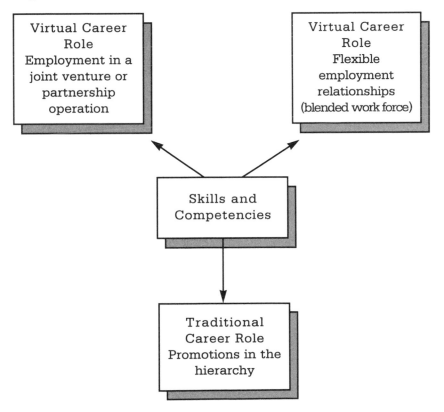

stagnant and people move from job to job. Second, jobs in a hierarchy are rationed to candidates. For each job opening, there may reasonably be more than one candidate. In order to maintain flexibility and meet the challenges of the new competition, alternative career paths need to replace the traditional approach.

Two alternatives have arisen with the emergence of the virtual workplace. The first is a virtual role related to employment in joint ventures and partnership relationships. This approach is in response to multi-company relationships established in managing the value chain. This role is most prevalent in the frontline and cyberlink virtual workplace models. It includes the breadth and depth of technical and team skills in very broad roles such as frontline sales and service and very broad natural team roles encompassing a whole process. Even in the most basic virtual relationship associated with the telecommuting model, the flexibility and self-discipline required point toward a virtual career role.

The second alternative relates to a flexible employment relationship we alluded to in Chapter 1 when we introduced the blended workforce. In the blended workforce, companies extensively utilize assignment or temporary employees and outsource skills that are not central to the competitive advantage of the organization and can be done best by others. The blended workforce is an essential component of the virtual workplace because it provokes companies engaged in a work process to accomplish two very important things. First, it provides flexibility relative to the ups and downs of the competitive environment as well as the highest-quality skills available on the open market almost instantaneously. Second, at the same time, it requires more sophisticated coordination and integration of the outsourced skills into the process. We will explore the blended workforce in Chapter 7.

What Does a Career Path Look Like in the Virtual Workplace?

If a career in the virtual workplace is not a succession of jobs, what does it look like? In the virtual workplace, careers are based on the foundation of skills and skill blocks that are the basis for work design. The breadth and depth of skills define the scope of the career path. Skills are additive. Once you master a skill, you continue to utilize it in some shape or fashion. The skill matrix introduced in Chapter 3 is the basis for the skill path. Figure 5.10 provides an example of a sales and technical service career path for the frontline model. In this model all members of a sales and service team are required to develop "core" skills and entry-level skills across all sales, service, support, and team functions. Each block takes approximately six months to master. Accomplished and advanced skills take one year each. Career paths are customized for each team member. The lighter boxes in Figure 5.10 represent technical service and customer service depth. The total for the career path is seven years.

Over a period of time, the skills are additive for each member of the organization, unit, or team. Once all the skills are mastered by the team, the process can be managed effectively.

Example of Career Paths for a Cyberlink Workplace

Smith & Nephew Orthopedics,[1] a leading manufacturer of human hip implants, restructured its manufacturing facility in order to increase the speed of manufacturing and provide extraordinary customer service to physicians and medical/hospital buying groups. Career paths changed from traditional manufacturing job hierarchies to integrated manufacturing teams. Figure 5.11 outlines the basis for multiskilled work teams at Smith & Nephew Orthopedics. As shown, every manufacturing associate is expected to possess seven core skills: applied mathematics, reading, applied technology, listening, teamwork, writing, and locating information. Note the breadth of the core skills required. Associates will also be expected to possess entry-level proficiency in every one of the seven skill block areas: material deployment, machining, finishing, packaging, maintenance, quality, and team skills.

Figure 5.10 Sales and Technical Service Career Path Example

Skill Level	Sales	Technical Service	Administration	Customer Service	Support Services	Team Skills	Time Frame
Advanced		Specialty		Specialty			12 months
Accomplished		Specialty		Specialty			12 months
Entry	Core	Core	Core	Core	Core	Core	6 months

■ Core Skills (required of all team members)

▨ Specialty Skills (required in a technical and customer service career path)

Figure 5.11 Skills and Skill Development Steps

Skill Level

	Material Deployment	Machining	Finishing	Packaging	Maintenance	Quality	Team Skills
Advanced							
Accomplished							
Entry							

Core Skills	Applied Math	Reading	Applied Technology	Listening	Teamwork	Writing	Locating Information

Since every manufacturing associate must have the basic skills and an entry-level proficiency for each skill block, distinct career paths become combinations of accomplished- and advanced-level skill proficiencies. Figures 5.12 through 5.14 illustrate skills/proficiency acquisitions for three career paths: material deployment, machining, and finishing. These career paths give frontline workers the opportunity to direct their careers and to master many skills. They also support self-managed teams that provide associates with autonomy and responsibility on the shop floor.

Depending on the process category, associates may increase their skills to the accomplished or advanced level. For example, packaging and maintenance contain only entry-level proficiency; material deployment, machining, and finishing have a progression of proficiency levels through the advanced level.

Of special importance are team skills, which relate to the development of the team system. These competencies include communication, team management, and supervision. Smith & Nephew has made acquisition of these skills a requirement for associates' career progression (and skill-based compensation).

The New Deal for Skills and Competencies

Companies that have moved toward the virtual workplace have immediately recognized the significant cost of developing the required skills. In response, they have really been forced to restructure the employment relationship around the New Deal as they have faced the virtual workplace. Based on the need to clearly define and set expectations about who is responsible for skill and competency, four different approaches to development have emerged: foundation competencies, core competencies, support competencies, and outsourced competencies (see Figure 5.15).

Foundation Competencies

Foundation competencies are those "tickets into the ballpark" which prospective employees must supply to the em-

Figure 5.12 Material Deployment Career Path

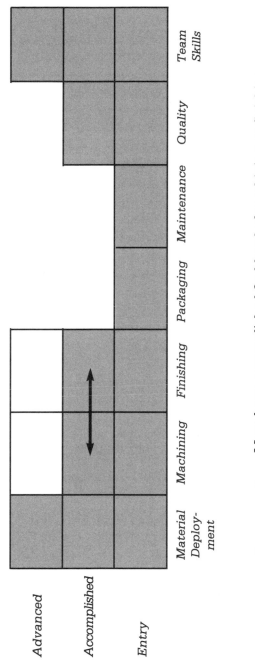

Skill Level

Advanced

Accomplished

Entry

Material Deploy-ment   Machining   Finishing   Packaging   Maintenance   Quality   Team Skills

→ Must have accomplished 2nd level of machining or finishing

Figure 5.13 Machining Career Path

Skill Level	Material Deployment	Machining	Finishing	Packaging	Maintenance	Quality	Team Skills
Advanced		▓					▓
Accomplished	▓	▓	▓				▓
Entry	▓	▓	▓	▓	▓	▓	▓

Must have accomplished 2nd level of material deployment or finishing

Figure 5.14 Finishing Career Path

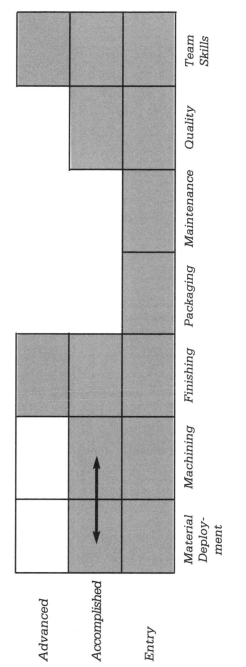

Skill Level

Advanced

Accomplished

Entry

Material Deploy-ment Machining Finishing Packaging Maintenance Quality Team Skills

← Must have accomplished 2nd level of material deployment or machining →

Figure 5.15 Skill and Competency Requirements

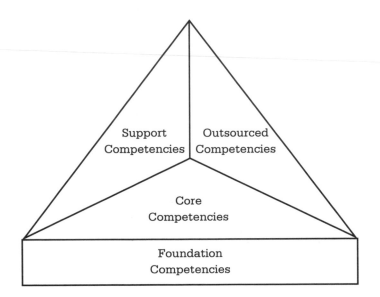

ployer because they will be required for them to function in the virtual workplace. Foundation competencies are critical capabilities in basic math, reading, and problem solving, as well as basic mechanical skills related to large and small motor activities (if required for manual skill work). Many problems have surrounded foundation competencies in organizations that have gone through restructuring and process redesign. When single-skilled employees are required to engage in high-performance teams, we often find that they do not have the basic social, technical, and/or motor skills necessary to learn and develop in these broadened roles. The companies that are attempting to make these changes basically have two alternatives:

1. *Invest in foundation competencies.* For example, Smith & Nephew was undergoing a change from traditional manufacturing to virtual, team-based manufacturing processes. In the future, semi-skilled employees as well as machinists and me-

chanical specialists would be cross-trained to work in teams in a just-in-time manufacturing environment. All members of the workforce were tested in basic skills ranging from reading and applied mathematics to basic teamwork and writing skills. Before the change could take place and before the new team members could begin training in manufacturing process skills (such as computer assisted machining), approximately 65 percent of the workforce had to complete foundation skill training.

2. *Select for foundation competencies.* Facing an enormous gap between employees' current capabilities in these foundation skills and those required in the future, many companies determine that many current employees will not be able to operate in the new environment. Many companies we have worked with subject the workforce to an assessment process to determine those who have the basic skills to operate in the new organization. Those who meet the basic requirements in the new work organization are offered positions and the opportunity to obtain training and development in the new field sales and service skill sets. Those who do not are redeployed in other areas of the company.

In the future, companies that wish to restructure in the virtual workplace will face immense training and development requirements. We expect that the developmental focus will be "core" skills (described below) rather than more generalized foundation skills. We predict that foundation competencies will be required as a condition of employment and that prospective employees will need to invest in their own careers by developing their own foundation competencies and presenting themselves to companies that require them.

Core Process Competencies

Certain critical competencies required by business processes are central to success of the company because they enable the company to derive competitive advantage. They include skills that the company will offer through in-house training and development. Employees who are involved in core skill tracks would expect and be provided with longer-term employment opportunities.

Core competencies are the skills and capabilities directly related to the work process itself. Core competencies of the company translate directly to core competencies of the individuals, groups, and teams that are driving the strategy of the company. Companies that have concentrated on restructuring and moving to a process redesign in recent years have redefined their core competencies as a central element of the restructuring process. For example, a company in the consumer electronics catalog distribution business would probably define one of its core processes as those activities related to a seamless order fulfillment process that begins with placing an order and ends with the receipt of a product on time that works when you plug it in the first time. This core process may include many activities across many internal departments such as order entry, customer service, warehousing, and distribution. However, *many activities in these "departments" may not be included in core processes*. In defining core processes and core skills that support those core processes, it is most effective to use the eye of the paying customer and ask: What do potential and current customers see as core or critical? What skills are demanded by customers?

The skills that are considered core are those that companies will focus on training and developing, building on foundation skills. The consumer electronics distribution company, for example, would concentrate on developing skills in its core process— the order fulfillment process that begins with the customer requesting information or actually ordering a product and ends with delivery of the product.

Individuals in the labor market seeking a long-term relationship with an employer will be most efficient in their job search if they focus on the following two criteria:

1. *Foundation skills.* Look for job opportunities with companies that require foundation competencies that you have developed through schooling or actual job experience.

2. *Core skills*. Seek job opportunities with companies whose core skills match up with your career path interests. In other words, if you are interested in a long-term employment relationship, go to work for companies favoring your interests.

Support Competencies

Support competencies are enablers of core skills that are critical for operations but not central to the mission and strategy of the organization. Employees in support skill tracks are subject to changes in the business cycle and should take greater responsibility for their employment and risk situations. Support competencies are complementary to core processes. We should not, however, confuse support processes with a traditional department. For example, information systems may be a support process; however, certain activities in the information systems department, such as technology development, may be an element of a core business process. What is a support competency in one company (e.g., McDonald's) might be a core competency in another (e.g., Microsoft).

Support competencies are important enough for a company to staff individuals as employees. However, the company should not invest as heavily—if at all—in the long-term development of staff in support roles. We would not expect significant training and development resources devoted to support competency career paths. In addition, we would expect a flexible workforce in support areas. With fluctuations in demand or season, we would expect to see the flexing of the support workforce with temporary or contract employees.

Outsourced Competencies

Sometimes competencies can be provided most effectively by those outside the organization. Individuals in outsourced tracks are employed by outside vendors, but they will work alongside those in core and support tracks. Outsourcing has become a very prominent approach to flexible staffing. The list of outsourced competencies may include food services, facility services, security, information systems, desktop publishing, benefits management, and records management. They are outsourced because they are considered "generic" enough to be managed by a third party. Any additional backup skills to complete tasks are supplied by the third party. Obviously, there is no real "deal" with the host employer regarding an employment relationship because the employment relationship is with the third party.

Skills and Competencies in Virtual Organizations: What We Have Learned

With the recent boom in popularity of competency-based pay systems, many companies have developed competency models based on strategic or individual skills. Our experience suggests that, while strategic and individual competencies are critical to understand and develop from an organizational perspective, process competencies represent the best platform on which to develop work systems. Strong strategic competencies allow a company to develop a strong sense of what it is and what it is not, thereby enabling it to achieve distinct competitive advantage. However, due to the intangible nature of most strategic competencies on a daily basis, strategic competencies should serve as the foundation upon which an organization is built (versus the infrastructure that allows work to be accomplished). Strong individual competencies allow companies to develop an employee population focused on common goals and outcomes through complementary behaviors and human qualities. In measuring performance, however, behaviors become secondary to real performance. Regardless of our attitude, our flexibility, or our tendency to innovate, we must deliver results. As such, individual competencies should allow us to determine the desired attributes of our workforce (versus the metrics upon which we base success). Process competencies remain the most effective tool to link strategy, behavior, and output on a daily basis.

Note

1. N. Fredric Crandall, Marc J. Wallace, Jr., and Daniel Bisgeier, "Team Pay Case Studies: Work & Rewards Redesign at Smith & Nephew," *Compensation and Benefit Review*. Special Report, 1997.

6

Rewards in the
Virtual Workplace

A client of ours faced a crisis. The company, a manufacturer of decorative wallcovering products, had 80 percent of its sales concentrated in four large customers—and they were angry. They issued the following ultimatum: Drastically reduce cost, certify perfect quality, and service just-in-time inventory systems by delivering the products in a twenty-four-hour window rather than on a two-week delivery cycle.

Clearly, radical reinvention of the company's processes was called for. The alternative was to go out of business. The senior leadership group of eight executives recognized the gravity of the situation. The problem was that eight hundred other people had no clue. And the present state of blissful ignorance was reinforced by the way they were paid:

• *The base pay system was modest and predictable.* Everyone in the same pay grade made the same amount of money. In addition, there were many pay grades. Finally, base pay movement from year to year was very predictable. Every employee had become accustomed over the last twenty years to receiving an increase that pretty much kept pace with inflation.

• *Production employees (engaged in making the product) were paid on a piece rate incentive system.* Under the program, an industrial engineer analyzed the job and judged how many piece parts (units of product) a worker under normal circumstances and at a normal pace should be able to produce. A piece rate incentive of $ .25 per piece was established for any additional piece parts produced in the hour. The standard had not changed in the past twenty years, and the average production employee was earning $9.00 per hour in base wages and an additional $6.00 per hour under the piece rate system.

Under the circumstances, the reward or compensation system was sending the wrong message. Rather than signaling that a wolf was at the door, posing a dire threat to the business and jobs, the pay system was reinforcing a false sense of security best summarized by the Bobby McFerrin hit, "Don't Worry, Be Happy."

Our case underscores three key principles about the role of rewards in the virtual workplace:

1. How we reward sends clear messages about a company's circumstances, direction, values, and goals.
2. The message received by rewards will have a long-term impact on what people do and don't do. Simply put, people will act and perform in ways that get rewarded. They will not act and perform in ways that don't get rewarded.

   Thus, the reward encouraged workers at our client's company to produce quantity even at the cost of quality. In addition, focusing on quantity at each step of production created huge amounts of work-in-process inventory, making the overall operation of the plant inefficient and driving up product cost.
3. How we reward represents a powerful opportunity (missed in our case) to teach the business and continuously improve performance on key business metrics.

In this chapter we will explore rewards in the virtual workplace. First we will define the scope of rewards systems and their role in the virtual workplace. Next we will review how rewards strategy provides structure to the total rewards system. We will then take a close look at base and variable pay. Finally, we will review indirect compensation in the virtual workplace.

Rewards, the Virtual Workplace, and the New Deal

Rewards are central to succeeding in the virtual workplace. In Chapter 1 we showed how the advent of the virtual workplace requires a New Deal for employment. The New Deal creates a compact between organizations and employees, setting new assumptions about the terms and conditions of the employment relationship and defining what each party should expect. Thus, how we reward will define the relationship between employer and employee in the virtual workplace. Research and experience demonstrate that rewards are important components of any deal between the organization and its employees.[1]

For the employee, rewards:

- Define one's relationship with the organization.
- Define self-worth to the organization and in the external marketplace.
- Symbolize relative levels of professional achievement and contribution.
- Provide the means for achieving and sustaining levels of well-being (e.g., food, shelter, education, lifestyle).
- Provide comfort in their presence and anxiety in their absence. ("Money," according to a French proverb, "can't buy happiness but it can soothe the nerves."[2])
- Constitute the major way of "keeping score" in a culture that likes to keep score and encourages individual achievement. In this sense, rewards make the game interesting.

Rewards present major opportunities for the organization to:

- Teach and communicate about the business.
- Attract and retain the kind of talent necessary in the virtual workplace.
- Shape and develop the competencies required in the virtual workplace.
- Continuously improve performance on key metrics at the individual, team, group, and organizational levels.

Of all areas of human resource practice (staffing, employee relations, training, and development), rewards will be the most critical in the virtual workplace because they are the crucible in which the New Deal is struck.

Rewards Defined

Rewards refers to all terms and conditions defining the relationship between an organization and its employees. Figure 6.1 illustrates the major components of rewards.

Total Rewards defines the universe or entire deal relating employer to employee. Within Total Rewards are *direct* and *indirect compensation*.

Direct Compensation

Direct compensation consists of cash directly paid to the employee in exchange for his or her work. Included in this category are:

- *Base pay*—the hourly wage or weekly/monthly salary earned.
- *Base pay progression*—movement of base pay over time, from year to year.
- *Variable pay*—incentive or bonus pay that does not fold into base pay. Such earnings may be based on perfor-

Figure 6.1 Total Rewards Components

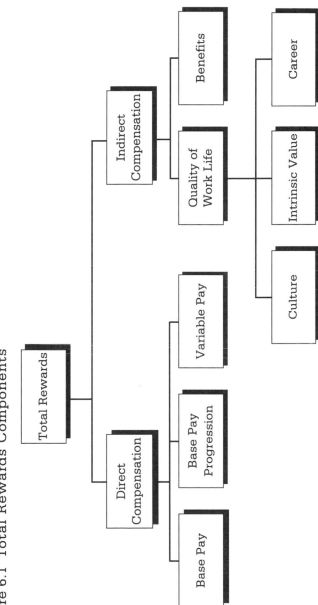

mance against preset goals (incentives) or paid at the discretion of the company (bonuses). Such earnings may be paid at the individual, team, group, or organizational level.

Base pay, base pay progression, and variable pay add up to total cash compensation paid in any given year.

Indirect Compensation—Benefits and Perquisites

In addition to direct cash, compensation is also paid in the form of indirect cash or benefits that have monetary value. Common benefit packages today include:

- Contributions to retirement plans and other forms of deferred compensation.
- Contribution to health insurance coverage.
- Life insurance.
- Legally required contributions, including Social Security and Medicare.
- Perquisites such as health club memberships and cellular phones.

Indirect Compensation—Quality of Work Life

Total Rewards also includes a broad array of non-monetary, but extremely important, rewards that we place under the general umbrella of *quality of work life* (QWL). Components of quality of work life include:

- *Organizational culture*—the norms and values defining appropriate behavior in the organization. One of the single most important cultural expectations we encounter today is employees' confidence in the business and its leaders. Quality of leadership and supervision are also defining elements of culture.

- *Intrinsic value*—rewards inherent in the work itself. These rewards come from the act of performing. Among such outcomes are how inherently interesting one's work is, the degree of variety experienced, the degree of autonomy and control over one's work, and the significance of the work to the business and its customers.

• *Career opportunity*—the prospects for development and growth. "What are my prospects? Where can I expect to be five years from now?" The answers to these questions are important for both organizations and employees. For organizations, careers represent the most efficient way to grow the talent they will need to compete as virtual organizations. For employees, careers represent valued opportunities to grow and achieve professional and occupational goals.

Our definition of Total Rewards is broad by design. Each element of Figure 6.1 represents a block for constructing the reward architecture required by the New Deal.

Total Rewards Strategy

Getting from building blocks to architecture requires a reward strategy. A strategy is a game plan for achieving some goal. In this case, moving from a traditional to a virtual workplace will require us to pay attention to rewards strategy.

Rewards Strategy Components

Rewards strategy has two components:

1. *Objectives*—defining the goals for rewards or, put another way, what we want to accomplish with rewards. Following are the most frequently cited goals by organizations making the transition from a traditional to a virtual workplace:

• Attraction and retention—attracting and retaining key talent.
• Communication—teaching the business by generating line of sight between individuals and key business metrics.

- Development—shaping the competencies required by the business and reinforcing business performance achievement.
- Contribution to performance—ultimately, organizations should expect rewards to contribute directly to improved business performance by reinforcing the contributions of individuals, teams, and groups.

2. *Architecture*—how reward building blocks fit together in order to achieve the objectives just enumerated. Architecture must define two components:

- *Design*—what the building blocks will look like (for example, base pay, variable pay, and benefits).
- *Operation*—how each reward component will work (for example, participation and payout in an incentive program).

When leaders think about total rewards as outlined above, it is a clear sign that they are getting strategic about rewards. Traditionally, companies have not viewed rewards strategically. Rather, they have viewed compensation merely as a cost of doing business, much as one would consider utilities such as electricity, water, and heat.

A virtual workplace, in contrast, demands that rewards become drivers of performance metrics such as revenue growth and profitability. Thus, we come to view rewards not as a cost but as an investment in performance. Consistent with such thinking was the response of the executive committee of a communications company to recommendations made to them regarding their rewards program:

"Last year we spent $1.3 billion on base wages and benefits, up $70 million from the previous year. Our revenues remain flat, we lost market share, and profits declined 10 percent. What did we get for the $1.3 billion in terms of enhanced competitive and organizational capability? What did we get for the additional $70 million?

"Last year, beyond base wages, we spent another $100 million on various incentives and bonuses. What did we get for that expenditure in terms of performance?

"The total compensation of $1.4 billion represents 60 percent of our total costs of $2.3 billion and 56 percent of our revenues of $2.5 billion. How can we harness compensation to improve both revenue growth and profitability?"

Such questions rarely arise in a traditional workplace because rewards are viewed primarily as an administrative or overhead cost. A virtual workplace, on the other hand, requires that we hold the money spent on rewards accountable for continuous improvement in business performance.

Role of Reward Strategy

If the communications company in our example is to realize a return on its rewards expenditures, it must begin to view rewarding people as a business process and it must gain control over that process. Rewards strategy is the tool to gain such control. Developing and executing a rewards strategy achieves the following:

- Gains control over the process of rewarding, directing it toward the goals we have set for the process (for example, teaching the business and generating exceptional customer satisfaction).
- Raises our sights or expectations for rewards from cost to investment in performance.
- Provides a yardstick for assessing the effectiveness of our current reward practices, allowing us to diagnose gaps or areas needing significant change.

- Provides benchmarks for identifying what improved reward systems will look like.
- Provides us with the architecture describing detailed blueprints for rewards systems and programs that will serve us much better in a virtual workplace.

The total rewards strategy required for the virtual workplace to function is quite different from that appropriate in a traditional workplace. These differences are illustrated in Figure 6.2. The differences require organizations to fundamentally rethink rewards strategy when transforming into a virtual environment.

We have found the analysis illustrated in Figure 6.2 to be an extremely valuable tool for executives in considering rewards strategy. Following the steps requires one to first establish the message our current systems are sending. Comparing the current message with the desired message in a virtual workplace will identify gaps in reward practices. Thinking about changes in rewards (base pay, base pay progression, variable pay) is the first step toward redesigning to support performance in the virtual workplace.

Figure 6.3 (on page 159) contains a template for you to use in conducting such an analysis in your organization.

Base Pay and Base Pay Progression in the Virtual Workplace

A consideration of base pay in the virtual workplace requires a stern look at the role of jobs and how it will change.

The Central Role of the Job in the Traditional Organization

The idea of a job is so central to our thinking about work that it is difficult, even counterintuitive, to consider what the workplace would be without it because:

Figure 6.2 Traditional vs. Virtual Messages

Reward Component	*Traditional Message*	*Virtual Message*
Base pay +	"This is the relative value of your job based on external labor market survey comparisons and internal job evaluation."	"This is the value of the personal skills and capacities you bring to the organization."
Base pay progression +	"This represents one more year with the company."	"This represents the greater depth and breadth you have added relative to our core business processes."
Variable pay =	"This is a privilege of membership, typically restricted to executives, managers, and salespeople."	"This is your share, as a business partner, in our success as a business."
Total cash compensation +	"Here's what you're entitled to."	"Here's what you have earned."
Benefits +	"Don't worry, we've taken care of it."	"We're sharing risk and accountability as business partners."
QWL +	"Do what you're told. We need your labor—not your ideas."	"We need your mind and involvement. You are empowered to make decisions."

(*continues*)

Figure 6.2 (*continued*)

Reward Component	*Traditional Message*	*Virtual Message*
Career opportunity	"Stay loyal and you'll have a job for life."	"You and the company are mutually responsible for your career. We will offer opportunity as business demands. You must constantly renew and grow your skill set."
=		
Total rewards	"This is what you are entitled to."	"This is your share of success as a business partner."

- We talk of work in terms of "jobs."
- We organize work activities into jobs and call them job classifications.
- We recruit and select people with a job in mind.
- People own jobs. One's identity is defined by the job one holds.
- Power and authority in organizations stem from the job. (Senior managers are more powerful than junior managers.)
- People's careers are defined by job changes. True advancement comes only when one leaves a job behind and steps into a new job.
- Jobs are turf. You can't do my work if it's in my job description, nor can I do your work if it's in your job description. I can't take your job until you vacate it.
- Jobs are neatly bunched into functional silos in traditional workplaces. All engineering jobs, for example, are arranged hierarchically in an engineering department. All claims jobs in an insurance company are sorted into a claims department.

Figure 6.3 Current vs. Virtual Messages

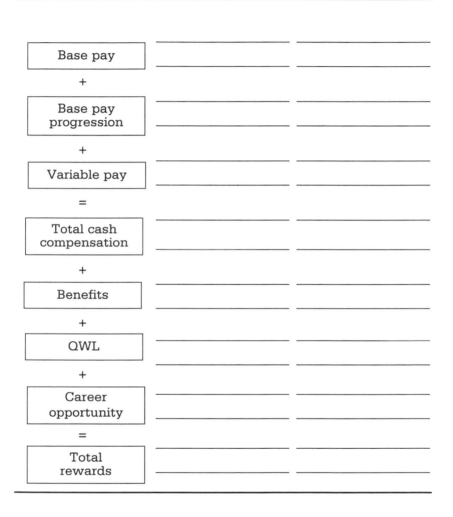

Reward Component	Current Message	Virtual Message

The Job and Base Pay

The job paradigm lies at the heart of human resource practices and has since the 1930s. Standard practice with regard to setting base pay and managing base pay progression required us to use the job as the unit of analysis:

- Market pricing practices force us to benchmark internal jobs with external jobs surveyed in external labor markets.
- Job evaluation methods have evolved since their inception in the 1930s as a tool to evaluate the relative worth of a job (often by assigning points to the job and assessing against a series of compensable factors).
- Jobs are sorted into hierarchically arranged pay grades, each with a minimum, midpoint, and maximum within which the employee's base pay must remain so long as he or she holds the job.

The first rule in evaluating a job is to think of the job, not the person who occupies the job. In a traditional workplace, then, one's base pay level is determined by the job one holds. Base pay progression is limited to the range of rates defining one's job pay grade. Modest increases in pay may be based on annual merit reviews, but the empirical data show that most people in a given pay grade rise with the same tide of annual structural or market-driven adjustments. Significant pay movement requires promotion to a higher job in a functional hierarchy.

Jobs serve traditional organizations well. Work is organized in a command-and-control bureaucracy characterized by functional specifications and hierarchy. It is a paradigm shaped by the early twentieth-century thinking of Max Weber and Frederick W. Taylor, implemented by Henry Ford, and cast in the legislation of Franklin D. Roosevelt's New Deal of the 1930s.

Unfortunately the paradigm no longer serves us because the job has died.

Death of the Job

Globalization of production and technological revolution—the two forces we explored in Chapter 1—have forced us into a post-industrial model for producing goods and service. The work designs of the virtual workplace (described in Chapter 4) have forced companies to tear down hierarchy, do away with functional specialization, and organize all activities according to entire business processes that cut across traditional departments and occupations.

A traditional insurance company, for example, has over four hundred job classifications, distributed across ten separate departments, and organized into as many as thirty pay grades.

A virtual insurance company, in contrast, will have ten to fifteen work matrices. The traditional hierarchy is steep (perhaps eight management levels), while the virtual hierarchy is flat (perhaps three to four levels). In the process, the job has died, and its death raises difficult questions about traditional base pay practices.

The experience of an insurance company introducing virtual products illustrates the challenge. Prior to the transition, insurance operations were segmented by functional silos. Sales represented accepted applications, underwriting evaluated the risk, and policy service issued the accepted policy. The score card: two weeks' cycle time, high cost, and many handoffs. The virtual work design created full-service teams consisting of fifteen people each that cut across sales, underwriting, and policy issue, as illustrated in Figure 6.4.

Rose was a member of the new team. In the former organization she had been assigned to the policy issue department at an annual salary of $30,000. Now her role was different. Her job had disappeared. She now occupied a role (represented by the shaded blocks in Figure 6.4) that required much more breadth and depth. In fact, she was now dealing with customers and participating in the sales and underwriting process (within specified limits). The adjustment was not easy for Rose. For one thing, she had a lot more to learn. For another, she had to take risks and make decisions that used to be made by people superior to her.

One day she had a question for her team leader: "Tom, I made $30,000 and I was OK with that. But now the company is asking me to take on a broader role. I know the other jobs are evaluated at higher pay grades and are more than $40,000. Are you going to pay me that?"

Clearly the answer is no. But what is the right answer?

Figure 6.4 Virtual Service Team

	Sales	Underwriting	Policy Issue	Policy Service	Team
Advanced			▓		▓
Accomplished			▓	▓	▓
Entry	▓	▓	▓	▓	▓

In another case, the research and development unit for a large high-technology firm faced a dilemma. The director wanted research engineers to broaden their value by gaining practical experience in the operations of the company. It seemed like a relatively straightforward choice to ask the engineers to take on assignments in the field. The problem, however, was that the only job open in the field was evaluated in a lower pay grade than the engineers' current job. Of course, the engineers took the assignment and, of course, they held on to their current pay. But the point is that the traditional job definition, job evaluation, and base pay practice constituted a barrier—something around which exceptions had to be made in order to do the right thing.

Virtual Base Pay

Both cases illustrate the need for a new base pay model—one that supports virtual work designs and one that does away with barriers.

In effect, the job has been replaced by a role, often on a team, that has much vaguer boundaries and requires greater depth and breadth of skills and abilities. Rose, for example, raised a valid point. Her newly acquired skills added to her personal worth to herself, her team, and her company. She didn't change jobs, but she changed her capacity to perform work. Consider the following: If Rose's capacity to perform customer service, underwriting, and expediting policies lowers unit cost by 30 percent, speeds cycle time from two weeks to one day, and results in loyal customers, has her personal asset value to the company increased? The answer is yes.

Paying the Person

Let's say Rose's company never had a formal job evaluation system, never even had jobs. Let's say it was a small, family-run operation of a pre-industrial age. The boss would have put Rose to work on some basic tasks. He'd want to run as lean as possible, so if Rose was capable of taking on more, he'd try her out. He'd also watch her progress. And he might even match her increased value (because of an increased ability to handle different parts of the operations) with increases in pay.

The simple picture from the past has become a reality in the virtual workplace. The differences between traditional and virtual workplaces regarding base pay is that a traditional company pays the job and a virtual workplace pays the person (see Figure 6.5).

The virtual workplace pays people not for the job they hold, but for the role they must play. The role is less formal, more flexible, and overlaps much more with other roles than did jobs.

Since jobs have disappeared, we can no longer determine a person's worth by asking what job he is assigned to now. Rather, we must ask, "What can he personally do for us?" The more of a business process he can perform effectively, the greater his value. The more valuable a person, the more we pay. This base pay is not constrained by job assignments and narrow pay grades. Rather, a person's growth in capacity to perform is matched by base pay increases until he reaches the full capacity needed by his team or organization and base pay reaches a target high rate representing fair market value for the skills and competencies he possesses. Such a system is called skill- or competency-based pay. The system is neither time-based nor annual. Fast trackers will move more quickly than others. Questions regarding merit pay shift from "How well has Joe done his job this year?" to "Is Joe making expected progress in developing and renewing the capacities needed in his role?"

Broad Pay Bands

The base pay structures that best serve a virtual workplace are a few broad pay bands. Each band manages the pay steps from entry to a target level. Bands are fewer in number and broader than traditional pay grades, as illustrated in Figure 6.6.

Figure 6.5 Base Pay Contrasted in Traditional vs. Virtual Work Designs

	Traditional	*Virtual*
Unit of analysis	Job	Personal role
Basis for value	Job evaluation	Personal evaluation
What pay is for	Work performed	Capacity to perform
Base pay progression	Modest movement within grades to mid-point. Pay is controlled to mid-point Promotion required for significant advancement	Significant movement from entry rate to target rate based on capacity acquisition
Base pay structure	Many narrow pay grades, hierarchically arranged	Few broad bands

Beware of Broad Bands

Broad bands are a hot topic today. Some companies have embraced them without sufficient forethought and have regretted the move. If many pay grades are merely replaced with fewer and broader bands, it should not be surprising to experience a rapid increase in wage rates and pressure on labor cost. Wages and salaries tend to drift to the top of the band. If such inflation cannot be justified economically, broad-banding has simply taken away the ability to manage labor cost. Broad-banding

Figure 6.6 Pay Grades vs. Pay Bands in the Virtual Workplace

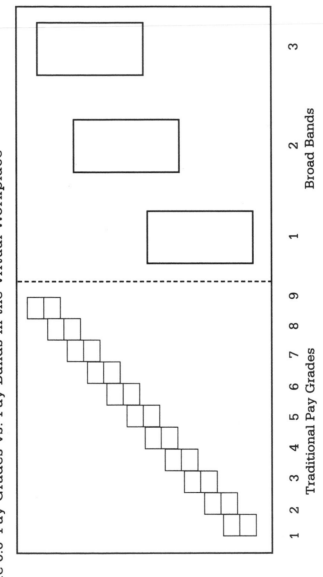

makes sense only when there is an economic justification for all employees to be at the target high rate for each pay band.

Skill- or Competency-Based Pay

The base pay progression policy that best serves the virtual workplace is skill- or competency-based pay. Under a skill-based system (as described above), a person's pay steps are matched to increasing skills or competency to manage an entire business process. A person enters the work design and role at an entry level of pay. He or she achieves a target high level once he or she is fully qualified.

Beware of Skill- or Competency-Based Pay

Skill-based pay is not for every company. It is expensive and it requires a substantial investment in training and development. Our research shows that an average company instituting skill-based pay experiences the following:

- 15 to 20 percent increase in wage rates
- 20 to 25 percent increase in costs of training and development
- Initial increases in head count and slack built into work schedules to allow people to cross-train and move around

Ten Hard-Won Lessons of Skill-Based Pay

Following are ten hard-won lessons from those companies who have succeeded with skill-based pay:

1. *Build the economic model first!* Using the tools presented in Chapter 8, develop an understanding of the fundamental economics underlying the work design. Be able to show how the work design will lead to additional economic value (for example, through higher labor productivity, faster cycle times, lower

unit cost, or lower inventory) so that it will more than offset the higher cost of the skill-based system.

2. *Be careful about what you call a skill or competency.* Competency has become an overused term and it applies to a wide range of uses, as we noted in Chapter 5. Let us be clear in what we mean by a skill or competency in the context of the virtual workplace. First, we are focusing on process skills that relate to economic value. Second, a *skill* or a *competency* must have the three components of knowledge, activity, and results (Chapter 5). Our definition of a skill covers all levels of work, from that of the CEO and senior executives to the operator on the floor.

3. *Be careful when drawing distinctions between a skill and a competency.* There is a temptation to draw a hard distinction between a skill and a competency. Skills are often perceived as narrow, tangible, and "lower level" tasks. A competency, in contrast, is often considered broader and related to higher-level, more strategic work.

Although this distinction has some face validity, it is dangerous and raises more confusion than it's worth. It has led some companies into the trap of maintaining the job evaluation system and hierarchies they have been trying to get away from. For example, skills would be the basis for valuing low-level, blue-collar, nonexempt work, while competencies would be reserved for higher-level, exempt, salaried, managerial work. Thus, skill-based compensation would become the province of blue-collar work. Salaried work would remain within the confines of traditional compensation programs, serving only to reinforce the system we need to move away from.

Our counsel is that a skill is a skill is a skill. The discipline of specifying knowledge, activities, and results applies at all levels of work.

4. *Don't pay for (reward) broadly defined traits.* The current market is awash with competency models that variously define competencies as (a) personality characteristics, (b) behavioral potential, or (c) general behavior patterns.

Certainly such characteristics are important in many work roles, but we are struck by the logic of the distinctions Nobel laureate Gary S. Becker[3] draws a line between general and specific learning. The broad traits we have just cited are what Becker describes as general learning. Such skills or competencies are general in nature and create value in many different settings. They are not unique to any organization. The key learning from Becker is that the value created by the application of general learning accrues directly to the employee. Therefore, the cost of acquiring and maintaining broad traits should be borne by the employee rather than the employer.

Our counsel is to treat broad traits as foundation competencies: those things you expect people to have as a condition of employment. Screen for them in selecting employees, and expect people to obtain them if they don't have them. Don't, however, pay incremental base pay for them.

5. *Watch out for "camping out."* The changes in work design required by the virtual workplace are not for everyone. Almost every time one of our customers reorganized work around processes, someone didn't like it.

The person often is a specialist, and perhaps has been doing the same job for fifteen to twenty years. He or she says, "I don't need more money; I'm happy to continue doing just what I'm doing—leave me alone!" The temptation is to do just that: "Let Mary camp out and we'll work around her." The problem with the solution, however, is that it creates dysfunction that detracts from process effectiveness. Working around Mary creates bottlenecks. Other team members don't get trained to do Mary's work. The result is high unit cost, slow cycle time, and lower quality.

We suggest adopting stern career and pay management policies. Employees are given ample time to adjust and achieve full capacity. If they do not make the change in the allotted time frame, they are then counseled into more appropriate roles or out of the organization.

6. *Make sure skill certification systems are user-friendly and valid.* One of the most frequent complaints we hear about skill-

based pay systems is that they are cumbersome. Team leaders complain about the volume of paperwork and the constant barrage of people seeking the next pay steps.

Keep things simple: institute windows (perhaps every three months) during which skill certifications occur. Involve people other than the team leader in assessment; for example, 360° procedures. Focus the assessment and certifications on the demonstration of observable results.

Finally, use timesaving software applications to ease the paper burden.[4] User-friendly software exists that allows the team leader to track members of the team, maintain progress in skill paths, and update certification and pay decisions.

7. Plan ahead for training and development resource requirements. When we ask clients who have introduced skill-based pay, "What would you have done differently?" near the top of everyone's list is, "We underestimated the training resources required." Make sure in planning that you make sufficient provision for:

- The training/development resources (instructors, materials) you will need
- Sufficient time for the employee to get to off-the-job and on-the-job training
- Sufficient slack in head count and schedules to allow people the flexibility to cross-train and learn

8. *Make sure that team leaders understand that performance management (not just appraisal) is one of their most important accountabilities.* Performance management is a continuing cycle that begins and ends with goal setting around performance and competency. The cycle includes ongoing coaching, performance assessment, performance development, teaching, and evaluation. The process of performance management should be job number one, where a team leader spends up to 80 percent of his or her time.

9. *Be ready when employees top out.* At some point all of us reach full capacity in our role. On some teams it might take three or four years, in other cases it takes longer. We are often asked by customers, "What do we say to the employee who reaches the target goals and asks, 'Is that all there is?'" We counsel that the best answer is, "Yes, that's all there is! Your pay represents fair market value for the skills you possess and are using in your role." There may also be the following additional rewards:

- Periodic adjustments to base pay reflecting external market movement.
- Promotion to a new role reflecting a substantial change in responsibility and competency, putting the employee in a new pay band.
- Variable pay opportunity based on team or individual achievement against goals (see our discussion of variable pay, below).

10. *Watch out for bottlenecks in the skill-based system.* Very often, organizations build unintended bottlenecks into their work designs. For example, assignments that everyone must experience create bottlenecks. The best way to avoid bottlenecks is to build enough time diversity and flexibility into skill paths. Allow for a variety of paths and opportunities to develop skills and put them to work.

Variable Pay in the Virtual Workplace

Historically, eligibility to receive variable pay was restricted to select groups of employees. Executive compensation, for example, has a history of short- and long-term incentives for senior managers, as does sales force compensation.

In recent years, increasing numbers of companies are extending variable pay opportunities to all employees. There are many reasons for this interest. One is a simple matter of moving compensation dollars from the fixed-cost category to the variable-cost category. However, many organizations have reasons beyond cost. They view variable pay as an opportunity to teach the business, raise employee line of sight to business performance, and reward employees for the contributions they have made to improvement in business performance. Finally, variable pay has become an attractive prospect for rewarding teams.

Variable Pay Defined

Variable pay is a reward that does not fold into base pay. It is a payment over and above base salary. We can distinguish among three types of variable pay:

1. *Incentive*—a cash payment that is earned when actual performance meets or exceeds a preset goal or standard. The key characteristic of an incentive is that there is a mutually agreed upon goal and award *before* the performance cycle starts. An example of an incentive would be a gainsharing or goalsharing program under which teams earn an incentive based on performance against unit cost and quality goals.

2. *Bonus*—a cash payment that is granted by management after the fact. The key feature of a bonus is that it is generally discretionary. An example would be a bonus paid on the evaluation of past performance, or a holiday bonus paid in December.

3. *Recognition*—a cash equivalent of value that is granted to recognize individual or group contributions or achievements. Most recognition awards are discretionary, although some may operate as incentives. An example would be a plaque presented to members of a project team recognizing achievement on a project.

The advent of the virtual workplace requires us to make careful design choices among the alternative methods for variable pay. In a traditional workplace, variable pay is not nearly as important. Performance standards are less well defined at the individual and group level and, therefore, variable pay tends to regress into an entitlement.

In the virtual workplace, work teams have become a critical way of getting work done. The virtual work designs described in Chapter 4 require process teams. Such an imperative creates a need to reward teams, and variable pay presents such an opportunity.

Variable Pay and Teams in the Virtual Workplace

Companies moving toward a virtual work design have experimented with teams as a way of restructuring the work itself. The following kinds of teams are found in virtual as well as traditional work design:[5]

• *Parallel team*—a group of people, each with a specialty, having a part-time commitment on a periodic basis for accomplishing or resolving issues. An example of a parallel team would be a standing committee to resolve labor grievances. The commitment to the team is part time and the work of the team is not the members' primary focus.

• *Project team*—a group of people with a full-time commitment to achieve some specific objectives. The team disbands after the project or moves on to the next project. An example of a project team might be a re-engineering task force assigned to implement a new customer service process.

• *Process team*—a group of people with a full-time commitment who work permanently on ongoing work. This is, perhaps, the most common manifestation of teams in the workplace. Examples include an automobile assembly team, a full-service insurance team, a surgical team, and an aircraft crew.

Before assigning a team variable pay it is critical to ask two questions: (1) What kind of team do we have? and (2) What are we asking the team to do? A parallel team, for example, usually represents a small part of an individual's work assignment. In addition, the members have heterogeneous skills (for example, accounting, engineering, clerical work, production work, and management). Variable pay is most likely not of high importance to such a team. Base and variable pay are driven more by each member's primary role and attachment to the organization. Thus, for example, managers on the team may participate in a management incentive program, while others on the team do not. Recognition and even bonuses might be appropriate for parallel teams, but they do not amount to a major part of each team member's compensation.

Project and process teams, in contrast, represent a full-time commitment from each member. The nature of the work, especially in process teams, binds the team members intimately. They must work in close collaboration to get the work done. In these cases, variable pay presents a powerful opportunity to reward and reinforce ongoing team performance. Incentives, as defined above, become a major part of compensation, oriented toward team accomplishment.

Unless we can definitively answer what we expect the team to accomplish, we do not have a solid basis for variable pay. Project teams and process teams generally have better defined expectations that relate directly to business performance. Thus, they make good candidates for variable pay. Figure 6.7 illustrates the major differences between parallel teams (characteristic of traditional organizations) and project and process teams in the use of variable pay.

Although we can find examples of parallel, project, and process teams in both traditional and virtual workplaces, process teams are far more characteristic of virtual workplaces. Thus, the opportunity of harnessing variable pay in a process team environment becomes an opportunity in the virtual workplace.

Teams, Process, and Variable Pay in the Virtual Workplace

Due to the interest in team pay, organizations are rushing to install incentive pay for all kinds of teams, creating some confu-

Figure 6.7 Variable Pay and Teams

Type of Team	Primary Reward Venue	Secondary Reward Venue
Parallel	Cash equivalent recognition	Bonus
Project	Project incentive	Cash equivalent recognition
Process	Process incentive	Cash equivalent recognition

sion. One company we are familiar with installed productivity incentives for several departments, and then transformed into teams on the basis of a re-engineering effort. The unintended result was that the "teams" competed against each other and withheld resources from each other in the interest of maximizing individual team results. The cost to the company was the reduction of overall business results.

Defining a team for pay purposes, therefore, is serious business. We noted in Chapter 4 that the key feature distinguishing the virtual workplace from the traditional workplace is a focus and organization around core business processes. If process is key to the virtual organization, then it must become the basis for defining teams, establishing performance standards for teams, and rewarding them.

Following is a simple set of three rules for accomplishing variable pay for process teams in the virtual workplace:

1. *The process defines the team.* Figure 6.4 shows a work design for a full-service insurance team driven by a business process. The process itself is diagrammed in Figure 6.8.

Note that the process has a trigger defined by a customer need and a conclusion defined by customer satisfaction. The in-

Figure 6.8 Process Map for Customer Fulfillment

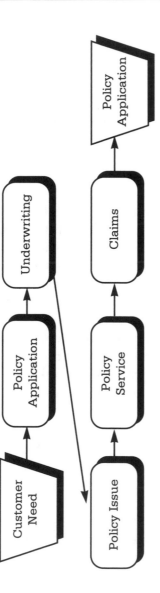

| Customer Need | → | Policy Application | → | Underwriting |
| Policy Issue | → | Policy Service | → | Claims | → | Policy Application |

Team Enterprise Report Card

	Goal	Actual
Unit cost		
Cycle time		
Error rate		
Customer satisfaction rating		

tervening process steps are those necessary to get from the trigger to the result. Anyone who touches the process and is necessary for the process to occur is defined as a member of the team. Thus, team membership cuts across traditional functional and occupational boundaries.

Defining the team in the virtual workplace is quite different from defining a team in a traditional organization. A virtual workplace requires that the team include the entire business process. Such a definition is quite a departure from traditional wisdom on teams in traditional organizations. For example, one common rule of thumb is that a team can be made up of no more than ten people. Yet Katzenbach and Smith define a team as a group of people who share a common set of goals and are held *mutually accountable* for their accomplishment.[6] We agree. In the virtual workplace, however, the goals are defined by the process and each team member's shared accountability is set by goals defined at the process level—not the department level or the small group level. Thus, the team so defined may include many more than ten people. Traditional rules of thumb for defining teams have been made irrelevant by the virtual workplace.

2. *Process metrics define the team's report card for incentives.* All business processes can be measured. Such metrics become the basis for measuring performance and setting goals. The enterprise report card illustrated in Figure 6.8 captures four key metrics for the customer fulfillment process: (a) cost, measured by the unit cost of each transaction; (b) efficiency, measured by the cycle time to complete customer transactions; (c) quality, measured by the frequency with which errors are made in the transaction; and (d) customer satisfaction, measured in this case by customer satisfaction ratings.

One's choice of process metrics should be driven by a consideration of which measures of the process will drive overall business results. In this case, quality, cost, efficiency, and customer satisfaction are seen as drivers of the overall business goals embodied in the firm's strategy: profitability, growth in business, growth in market share, and customer retention.

3. *Goals for process metrics determine the team's goals.* Just as process metrics define a report card for the team, so do the goals set on those metrics become the goals to be achieved by the team. Research and experience in the virtual workplace show that the most effective way to set goals is to involve the team itself. Goals set by team members often are tougher than those set by upper management. In addition, the process of setting goals creates ownership of the goals and a commitment to achieve them.

Indirect Compensation in the Virtual Workplace

Figure 6.1 indicates that beyond direct compensation there are elements that involve indirect (non-cash) rewards or compensation. These include *quality of work life* and *benefits*. The advent of the virtual workplace and the New Deal creates major changes in these components as well. Figure 6.9 illustrates the major shifts that take place.

Culture

Shifting to the virtual workplace requires a shift from a top-down, command-and-control style of managing to high involvement. What makes the virtual workplace faster is the fact that people on teams who are closest to business processes make decisions on the run. They don't wait to be told what to do. They don't wait for others to make decisions for them. Management in the virtual workplace must be prepared to invest in human assets so that teams can make effective decisions.

Intrinsic Value

People don't get bored in the virtual workplace. Taking work beyond the bounds of traditional job and functional boundaries requires greater breadth and depth for everyone.

Figure 6.9 Indirect Compensation in the Virtual Workplace

Indirect Compensation Component	Traditional Workplace	Virtual Workplace
Culture	Top-down, command and control	High involvement, empowerment to make decisions
Intrinsic value	Single or restricted task jobs, repetitive, little or no line of sight	Greater breadth and depth of activity, great line of sight to entire business processes
Career	Guaranteed employment for life, if you stay local	No guarantees, employment as long as the business need exists
Benefits	Privilege of membership	Shared risk and accountability

Most employees find such arrangements more interesting and meaningful than traditional jobs. The inherent interest in participating in a business process is a significant reward—all by itself. In addition, we have had numerous employees report to us that they attach high reward value to being able to control results and make a difference. Finally, the virtual workplace allows employees to raise line of sight and understanding from single-task jobs to the customer.

Careers

In traditional workplaces there was an implicit deal that offered lifetime employment in exchange for loyalty. In the virtual workplace there will be no guarantees of a job. There will, however, be the prospect of meaningful career assignments related to business processes—as long as the business need exists. Careers in the virtual workplace, then, will be related more to an individual's maintaining and developing personal competencies needed by the organization than to any guarantee of a job based on loyalty.

Benefits

Benefits include a variety of protections, including retirement pension programs, health insurance, life insurance, disability insurance, and more. Since the 1950s, benefits have ballooned as a part of total compensation in traditional workplaces. Such rewards represent up to an additional 40 percent of base pay earnings for U.S. workers. We don't see benefits going away in the virtual workplace. We do forecast a major change in the way they operate and the way they will be financed.

We see benefits moving away from being an entitlement or privilege of membership. Increasingly we see employees in the virtual workplace being asked to share risk and accountability. Beyond joint employer and employee contributions to finance retirement (for example, 401k plans) and to provide health insurance (for example, co-payments and deductibles), there will be increased portability of programs. While these changes are taking place across all types of organizations, they will be pronounced in the virtual workplace.

What We Have Learned About Rewards in the Virtual Workplace

Rewards are the crucible in which the New Deal for work and rewards will be struck in the virtual workplace. Management cannot long afford to put off considerations about rewards when redesigning work. Rewards will play a key role in:

- Communicating that change is taking place and defining what will be expected of everyone
- Teaching the new business and raising everyone's line of sight to new business processes defining the virtual workplace
- Reinforcing and rewarding the changes in individual behavior and team performance that will be necessary to succeed in the virtual workplace

These changes don't just happen as natural events in the shift to the virtual workplace. Managers must develop explicit rewards strategies using the tools presented in this chapter.

Notes

1. Charles Fay and Marc Wallace, *Compensation Theory And Practice, 2nd ed.* Boston: Kent Publishing, 1990.
2. Ibid.
3. Gary S. Becker, *Human Capital, Third Edition*. University of Chicago Press, Chicago, 1993.
4. Center for Workforce Effectiveness has developed TeamTrack software available for review at www.cwelink.com.
5. Edward Lawler and Susan Cohen, "Designing Pay Systems for Teams," *ACA Journal*. Autumn 1992, Ii; 6–19.
6. Jon R. Katzenbach and Douglas K. Smith, *The Wisdom of Teams*. Harper Business, 1993.

7

The Blended Workforce

The *blended workforce* is a signature characteristic of the virtual workplace. It is defined as a mixture of employees from more than one company working on a common site. A traditional workplace, in contrast, includes all employees working for one company on one site and treated in the same way. In the virtual workplace you may walk through a facility and encounter employees working together, but for a number of employers. The work and rewards programs in these employee groups may also be different, including different management, hiring policies, compensation, and benefits. Companies have accommodated arrangements like this for over fifty years, going back to the colocation of government inspectors in manufacturing military industries in the Second World War. What is new and compelling about the blended workforce, however, is the strategic intent for adopting a blended workforce.

The blended workforce is a set of work and rewards arrangements that enables a company to execute competitive strategy through increased customer satisfaction, increased efficiency, and lower cost.

As we shall see, the blended workforce is an element of our most advanced virtual workplace—the cyberlink model. In this chapter we will explore the blended workplace in detail. First, we will describe its structure and elements. Next, we will describe how the blended workforce is a platform for the New

Deal. We will then provide a portrait of the blended workforce based on a sample of companies utilizing it. Finally, we will review work design, rewards, and skill and competency implications of the blended workforce.

The Many Shapes and Forms of the Blended Workforce

Contemporary North American companies have created assemblages of work groups in unique ways. Following are some combinations companies have created:

• Hitachi Computer Products (America), Inc., teams up with Kelly Services, Inc., in Norman, Oklahoma, to supply temporary assignment workers on production work teams. Kelly employees provide basic semi-skilled work in the facility and take up the slack in peak performance periods.

• Cessna teams up with Allied Signal in its single-engine aircraft assembly plant in Independence, Kansas. Allied Signal employees provide expertise in avionics and have on-site people who supply the avionics equipment for assembly on a just-in-time basis.

• The Bose speaker facility in Waltham, Massachusetts, maintains Ryder truck personnel on site. Lucent Technologies has Federal Express employees work on site in its Little Rock, Arkansas, facility. Co-location of transportation and manufacturing work results in more efficient and quicker delivery to customers.

Many companies that have undergone significant changes through re-engineering and restructuring have defined work in such a way that certain work is outsourced to third parties because other organizations are able to perform these services more efficiently and at a lower cost. As we noted in Chapter 4, certain skills associated with this work are defined as "core" skills. (For example, at Lucent and Bose, the core skills include manufacturing but do not include transportation.) These outsourced skills are then transferred to other companies who specialize in them. However, these activities need to be performed on site. Thus, the employees from the transportation companies move onto the assembly and manufacturing site. Such arrangements began with nonessential services, such as the cafeteria, but have moved to transportation, information technology, and human resources. Any service that can be done or can be considered to be done better by outsiders is a candidate for outsourcing. (Of course, some services can be contracted off premises as well; we have considered these in Chapter 2.) The blended workforce, however, is unique to a combination of people working for more than one company on a single site.

Another important outcome of restructuring is the reformation of the manufacturing process around regular and assignment employees. In this arrangement there is a longer-term investment in employees who receive training and development and career advancement opportunities. These workers either possess or are trained in the core skills. Assignment employees support the core by performing support work (even though the work itself may be of a more complex or higher skill level). Assignment employees may work on a part-time basis or freelance basis but are considered temporary, conducting assignments usually lasting a maximum of six months. Of course, the employees work on site. In the case of Hitachi, there is a third-party employer and the employees report to an on-site Kelly Services manager.

The Composition of the Blended Workforce

The use of assignment employees and outsourcing in earlier times mainly involved filling staffing gaps for vacations, fluctuations in seasonal production, or extraordinary projects (e.g., taking inventory in department stores). The demise of the career franchise and the need to be flexible in meeting customer demand have contributed to the rise of the blended workforce.

The blended workforce differs from earlier use of temporary employees. It is a structured but flexible mixture of full-time regular employees, temporary (or assignment) employees, and on-site employees who are working for another employer (third-party employees).

The latter two groups are not directly employed by the host company. Assignment employees are generally employed by an employment agency/temporary employment company. Contract employees may be part of a third-party company doing business on site (e.g., employees working for a contracted-out service, such as a cafeteria or handling finished product shipments for a distributor).

These arrangements are becoming a more compelling approach to employment because they provide flexibility around a steady core workforce during periods of fluctuating employment demand, and they allow the host company to concentrate on its core processes. Figure 7.1 summarizes the types of employees we are likely to see working together on a common site.

The Blended Workforce and the New Deal

The New Deal for work and rewards is built on the principle of customer-focused work processes. As we have pointed out, the explicit employment contract of a "lifetime job" is changing to one of a more explicit employment relationship defined by specific *required* skills. Thus, the blended workforce is a means by which a company can clarify the skills and employment relationships for the future.

The blended workforce is generally not structured uniformly throughout the organization. It has begun to take shape in the parts of companies that have undergone process redesign and restructuring and where there are highly concentrated numbers of employees. Indeed, the move to a blended workforce is a key mechanism that companies have used to bring restructuring down to the individual employee level. When manufacturing is restructured around core processes it is a natural next step to de-

Figure 7.1 Composite of the Blended Workforce

Type of Employee	Employer	Employment Arrangement
Full-time regular	Primary business on site	Full-time, full wage/salary and benefits package of host company
Temporary assignment	Employment agency	Part-time employee or temporary employee
Contract employee	Third-party contractor	Full-time employee working for the third party on site

fine a workforce that will work on a full-time regular basis and develop the capability to manage the process. Support processes are then candidates for outsourced work to a third party. Similarly, temporary or assignment employees are engaged to provide flexibility for additional assistance during peak periods, vacations, or other extraordinary circumstances. Figure 7.2 shows the relationship between core work, assignment work, and support work.

In *core work*, a company will employ core skills and invest heavily in developing the capability of its workers through training, career development, and performance management processes. Thus, it makes sense for core workers to be regular full-time employees. Flexible assistance, or *assignment work,* is provided in specific tasks and the skills required are basic or generic capabilities that the company can utilize on a part-time or periodic basis without investing in development of the employee. However, core work and flexible assistance are tightly integrated into the work flow. On the other hand, *support work* and skills are outside the main work flow and can be easily outsourced. When the work function is outsourced, employees generally work on site for another employer.

Figure 7.2 Building a Flexible Workforce Around the
Core Work

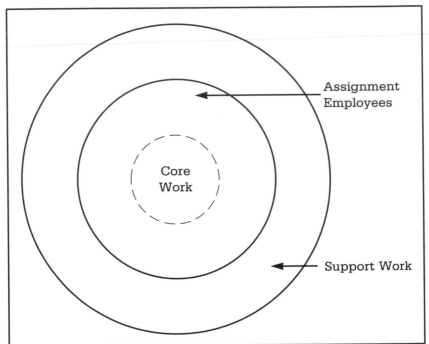

Because companies rarely completely restructure throughout, the blended workforce is usually a mixture of restructured
processes and parts of the company that are not restructured.
This can be confusing if there is not a clear understanding of
what areas will become restructured around core work, flexible
assistance, and support work. As a manager noted recently, "I
don't know if tomorrow I might get my pink slip and then be
asked to come back as a contract consultant."

The challenge to employers is to forge a completely blended
workforce which exists when all employees have clearly defined roles and career paths. For the foreseeable future it is un-
likely that such clarity and stability will reign in North
American organizations. But there is a palpable need to move in
that direction.

Challenges of the Blended Workforce

The blended workforce has created new challenges for work and rewards programs due to the mixture of employees on site. These employees work together for the same objectives on the same equipment in common processes—but because they are working for different companies, their pay and benefits will differ. Of special note are issues related to work design, staffing, and rewards:

• *Work design.* The blended workforce can create barriers between employee groups resulting in performance problems. For example, a "we" and "they" attitude may be reflected in a work process with regular and assignment employees. "We" are those employees who have a longer-term stake, possess more diverse skills, and are provided career opportunities. "They" are the assignment employees who are employed by a staffing agency. To avoid conflict and, more importantly, to promote the ongoing development of an effective work process, the organization must set clear expectations and take special care to overcome these barriers.

• *Staffing.* With a blended workforce, employees are hired through numerous sources and channels. Regular full-time employees are the "core" of the workforce. Core employees possess a wider variety of skills to support ongoing operations and provide a basis for continuity. Employees on temporary assignment or on contract will have a more arm's-length relationship with the business and its processes. Therefore, the host employer will need to staff the organization in a seamless way, "blending" the skills and competencies of regular and assignment/contract employees.

• *Rewards.* In a blended workforce, compensation programs should promote a single set of objectives and provide reinforcement for success on common goals. This will require compatible base pay and pay progression programs supporting skill development and individual performance for a common process, not withstanding the fact that the on-site employees may work for more than one employer. Similarly, variable pay programs should have a common set of measurements, universal participation, and common payouts. Such programs present numerous issues regarding design, funding, and legal complications concerning the use of common pay programs across employers.

A Portrait of the Blended Workforce

The portrait of the blended workforce is based on a sample of seventy-six heavy users of assignment and outsourced services in the United States.[1] A "heavy user" is defined as a company that utilizes on-site services and attempts to integrate all workers into the blended workforce model. Following is a description of the key characteristics defining the blended workforce.

Industry Profile

The blended workforce is most prevalent in manufacturing (49%), with a significant number in distribution (17%) and financial investment services (11%) as well. Figure 7.3 is a distribution of companies by industry.

Figure 7.3 Industry Profile

Industry	Percentage of Sample
Manufacturing	49%
Distribution/logistics	17
Financial/investment services	11
Technology	5
Retail/wholesale	4
Insurance	3
Other	11

Duration of Assignments

Longer-term assignments are more prevalent than short-term assignments. Two-thirds of companies using a blended workforce use assignment employees for long-term assignments (3 months or more), and one-third uses assignment employees for short-term assignments (less than 3 months). However, companies that use a greater number of assignment employees on site per week tend to use a greater percentage of the employees for short-term assignments, as indicated in Figure 7.4.

Type of Work Performed

Assignment employees generally do the same work as permanent or regular employees. An overwhelming majority, 84 percent, do the same kind of work. Assignment employees are utilized primarily in production/distribution/assembly operations and in clerical positions. See Figure 7.5.

Figure 7.4 Term of Assignment by Number of Assignment Employees on Site

	Number of Assignment Employees On Site		
Term of Assignment	*50 Employees*	*51–100 Employees*	*Greater Than 100 Employees*
Short-term (3 months or less)	20%	24%	32%
Long-term (greater than 3 months)	80	76	68
Total	100%	100%	100%

Figure 7.5 Types of Assignment Employees Utilized

Business Unit	Percentage of Survey
Production, distribution, and assembly	37%
Clerical, office automation	26
Customer service/teleservices	12
Information systems	8
Technical (e.g., drafting, engineering)	8
Professional (e.g., accounting, legal)	8
Total	100%

Assignment Employees as a Part of the Workforce

Overall, 24 percent (24%) of responding workforces are composed of temporary or assignment employees. The extent of blending varies by location. Manufacturing and corporate headquarters approximate the overall percentage. In customer service centers (Call Centers), assignment employees make up, on average, 39 percent of the workforce. Figure 7.6 summarizes the distribution of regular and temporary workers by location.

Team Participation

The majority of companies employing a blended workforce employ assignment employees in work teams (62%). Assignment employees typically have similar responsibilities to permanent employees on the teams. These teams range from production floor groups to customer service and process improvement teams.

Reception of Assignment Employees Into the Workforce

Overall, assignment employees are not seen as a competitive threat by core workers, as indicated in Figure 7.7. Barriers

Figure 7.6 Percentage of Workforce Comprised of Temporary vs. Regular Employees by Location

Location	Temporary	Regular
Overall	24%	76%
Manufacturing	25	75
Corporate headquarters	24	76
Regional/division office	14	86
Distribution center	20	80
Customer service	39	61

that employees can face are differences in qualifications and capability between the core and assignment employees that stir up distrust, competition, and poor working relationships. Of course, assignment employees in many cases, by design, do have a narrower scope of skills and less experience than core employees. Some differences in qualifications do exist. At the same time, there is a minimum of competition for jobs. The relative lack of competition that might be expected is based on the fact that with blended workforces there is a clear distinction among core and assignment career paths.

Blended Workforce Impact on the Organization

The use of a blended workforce has improved productivity and other key measures such as cycle time, cost, and customer service, as indicated in Figure 7.8. These results indicate that the blended workforce has a direct impact on the types of strategic objectives that lead to overall competitive advantage. In every case, the positive impact is significantly greater than the negative impact. There are many important improvements beyond the driving factor of cost control (71%). These positive results are attributable to the careful segmentation of the workforce into core and support elements and the methodical building up of a blended workforce.

Figure 7.7 Perception of Working Relationships

	Percentage Responding	
Working Relationships	*Yes*	*No*
Core and temporary workers see each other as coworkers and enjoy harmonious working relationships.	50%	50%
Core and temporary employees see each other as competing for the same jobs; working relationships are tense.	10	90
Temporary workers are seen as less qualified by core workers.	29	71

Figure 7.8 Performance Impact of the Blended Workforce

	Impact		
Improvement	*Positive*	*Negative*	*No Effect*
Improving productivity	64%	17%	19%
Reducing cycle time	51	11	38
Controlling costs	71	10	19
Improving customer service	52	12	36

Blended Workforce Work Design

Companies that have successfully employed the blended workforce have carefully segmented the workforce and defined explicit roles for core, assignment, and outsourced employees. Core employees are placed on career tracks with a structured set of opportunities for skill development and corresponding compensation. Boundaries are set for assignment employees relative to the skills utilized, work performed, and compensation opportunities. Similarly, the activities of outsourced functions are closely coordinated with core and assignment activities. The most critical elements to coordinate are core and assignment work roles because employees are engaged in a common work process.

The skill matrix utilized in the cyberlink workplace is an appropriate framework for the blended workforce because it defines work as a set of skills to complete a process. Figure 7.9 depicts a skill matrix for an electronics manufacturing company. Core employee career paths require approximately four years to complete and include four blocks. The first three blocks include mastery of a single process and the fourth is for an adjacent process. The example in Figure 7.9 includes Mechanical Assembly and Wire Harness Assembly processes. Assignment employees work only at the entry level. In times of great demand, a greater number of assignment employees are brought in and core employees focus on intermediate- and advanced-level work.

In order to maintain an effective work system, one with high motivation and the absence of competition, it is important to have clear roles for core and assignment employees. Career paths for regular core employees go a long way toward focusing regular employees' efforts. However, perceived competition for jobs may be a problem. The cause of competition may have many sources, including the lack of understanding by the core workforce of its own employment security, as well as real or perceived differences in background, skill, and knowledge between core, assignment, and contract employees.

Although companies using a blended workforce work on merging the cultural differences between the core, contract, and assignment employees, the turnover and disruption caused by short-term employees heighten concern about job security and stability within the ranks of core employees. As one employee noted, "When the time comes for the assignment employee to leave, it is looked at like a layoff by our core employees."

The work system must be managed to create clarity among

Figure 7.9 Electronics Manufacturing Skill Matrix

	Mechanical Assembly	Wire Harness Assembly	Manufacturing Preparation Activities	Soldering	Testing	Trouble-shooting
Advanced	▓					
Intermediate	▓					
Entry	▓	▓				

Core Employee Career Paths: Each career path is composed of four skill blocks. The first three are blocks focused on developing expertise in one area. The fourth is an entry-level block in another area that is included in the career path for flexibility and a broader base of knowledge. (The Mechanical Assembly career path is shaded.)

(continues)

Figure 7.9 (continued)

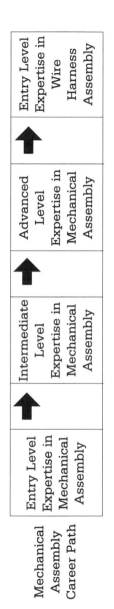

Mechanical Assembly Career Path	Entry Level Expertise in Mechanical Assembly	→	Intermediate Level Expertise in Mechanical Assembly	→	Advanced Level Expertise in Mechanical Assembly	→	Entry Level Expertise in Wire Harness Assembly

Assignment Workers: Assignment workers are expected to perform only entry-level activities. During heavy production periods, core team members will perform higher-level activities and an expanded assignment workforce will be employed to perform the majority of entry-level activities.

Career Path Completion Time: All career paths for core employees are expected to take 4 to 6 years to complete.

the various components of the blended workforce. Following are a number of management techniques that have been successful:

- Sole sourcing contracts for assignment employees with an on-site manager from the staffing company provides a clear line of authority and communication for assignment employees. In addition, it provides a consistent staffing function. If done effectively, the sole source contractor can provide a steady stream of assignment employees compatible with the ongoing requirements and culture of the host employer.

- Frequent one-on-one communication with contract and assignment employees regarding hiring opportunities for regular positions helps make the transition from "temp-to-perm" seamless.

- Inclusion of assignment employees in workplace events such as "all-hands" meetings helps bridge the information and culture gap of the core and assignment workforces.

- Inclusion of assignment employees on work teams helps to emphasize required teamwork and the company's work requirements. Even though assignment employees will probably play a limited role on work teams, they cannot be expected to work effectively if they don't know what their role is.

Blended Workforce Skills and Competencies

Skills and competencies will differ according to the work role. Regular or core employees will be offered the opportunity for a career path with a depth and breadth of skill covering the whole work process. Assignment employees will be expected to have skills focused on the entry level. Contract employees, on the other hand, will be expected to possess either entry or advanced skills in the particular outsourced specialty provided to the company.

The four types of skills and competencies that we introduced in Chapter 4 apply to the blended workforce.

1. *Foundation skills.*   Basic skills (such as mathematics and language) that enable an individual to acquire employment in the company and are used in all jobs.

2. *Core skills.*   Skills central to the main work of the company.

3. *Support skills.*   Skills that are not central to the company and are supportive to the core processes (such as accounting or human resources). The company maintains staff to complete these activities.

4. *Outsourced skills.*   Skills that are not central to the company and are performed better by experts on a contract basis.

Which skills are core, support, or outsourced will differ for each company based on its business strategy and operations. However, there are some clear directions for a company to take, as outlined in Figure 7.10. All employees need to have foundation skills in order to maintain employment. Core skills, of course, must be possessed by regular employees. Support skills may be required of regular and assignment as well as contract employees. This is because support skills may be required by all three groups in order to maintain maximum flexibility. Finally, outsourced skills are possessed by contract employees.

Rewards in the Blended Workforce

Compensation and rewards can integrate the blended workforce by sending clear messages and reinforcing behavior to drive work performance. Rewards programs will necessarily differ among core, assignment, and contract employees (see Figure 7.11), but together they should combine to support the economics of the workplace. (A fuller treatment of rewards is covered in

Figure 7.10 Blended Workforce Skills and Competencies

Skills & Competencies	Blended Workforce Element		
	Regular	Assignment	Contract
Foundation	X	X	X
Core	X		
Support	X	X	X
Outsourced			X

Chapter 8.) Figure 7.10 outlines the differences in base and variable pay for all three groups.

Rewards for Regular or Core Employees

Regular or core employees are long-term employees. The company is willing to invest in the development of these employees, and compensation programs reflect this longer-term orientation.

Base pay is designed around a career development program. Skill or competency-based pay provides a pay progression for acquisition of skill or competency blocks, as outlined in Chapter 6. Similarly, variable pay in the form of group incentives (goalsharing) provides a reward for achieving team and business unit objectives.

Rewards for Assignment Employees

Assignment employees work for a second party (e.g., a temporary employment agency). The duration of employment typically is six months and the work performed is generally localized to the entry level. Base compensation for assignment employees is generally a single rate for the duration of the assignment that is within the range of the entry-level rate of core or regular employees. For those companies that provide a "temp-to-perm" transition for assignment employees, it is critical that the rate for core and assignment employees be coordinated.

Assignment employees should be provided variable pay to support the efforts of the teams and the business unit. Because assignment employees work for a different employer, the performance measures for rewarding variable pay should be aligned with the support that is being provided to the host employer. Typical performance measures are consistency of attendance, productivity, quality, and customer service. The size of the award should be coordinated with the host employer's variable pay plan.

Rewards for Outsourced Employees

Outsourced employees generally work for a third-party employer or on a contract basis for the employer. While assignment employees work alongside core or regular employees, outsourced employees generally provide a separate function to the host employer. It is, therefore, fairly easy to identify the performance metrics of the service or function and develop performance incentives associated with the outsourced service. Thus, the most prominent element of the reward for outsourced services will become performance incentives. Base pay can be based on a contract sum for the duration of the contract, or, conversely, the contracting company will have its own base salary program.

Employee Relations Challenges in the Blended Workforce

Companies that have gone down the path of the blended workforce have faced formidable challenges related to workforce culture and organization. Following are some of the key challenges faced and how they have been overcome:

Figure 7.11 Blended Compensation Programs

	Regular	Assignment	Contract
Base pay	Skill-Based	Single-Rate	Contractor Salary Structure
Variable pay	Group incentive based on company metrics metrics	Group incentive based on company and/or agency	Group incentive based on contractor metrics

- *Equity of treatment.* Assignment employees typically earn lower wages, have a different (and reduced) benefits package, and may have a longer work week. This causes problems in maintaining a cohesive work environment.

- *Meshing of cultures.* Often assignment employees undergo a different hiring process than regular employees and have significantly different experiences, qualifications, and work life background than the core labor force. This also causes cohesion and communication problems.

- *Lack of involvment and motivation of temporary workforce.* Not being involved in the "core" of the business often leads temporaries to the periphery and to a lack of interest in the "bigger picture" of the company.

- *Pressure to move from "temp-to-perm."* Temporaries are often quite aggressive in desiring to move to regular positions, putting pressure on line management and human resources personnel.

Companies have employed many approaches to overcoming these challenges, leading to a successful arrangement. These approaches include:

- *Employ an on-site manager to deal directly with management issues of assignment employees.* Having an on-site manager is a major factor in making the blended workforce function effectively. The on-site manager should provide supervision of the employment relationship. In addition, the manager should counsel assignment employees on their performance and work behavior.

- *Manage the size of the temporary workforce.* The sizes of the temporary/assignment and contract components vary by company and by function. A mushrooming blended workforce can lead to many operations, performance, and human resource growing pains. The larger the assignment workforce becomes, the greater the requirement for effective management. Companies have dealt with this issue by having an on-site manager for assignment employees. Even with on-site management, however, as the assignment workforce grows it begins to have an impact on the host company culture. Therefore, other approaches to management we have recommended are required to maintain a focused and productive workforce.

• *Clearly communicate compensation, benefits, and employment policies.* All employees on site should have a clear understanding of the "deal" for all employees. This includes the differences in the salary and benefits package, the policy for continuation of employment, the "temp-to-perm" process, and other key policies. Additionally, there should be a clear explanation of why the company is adopting the policies and what the benefits are to everyone (e.g., employment opportunities for assignment employees, more employment security for regular employees, management of overtime, etc.).

• *Conduct ongoing education and training programs.* Technical skills training programs for assignment employees will result in higher-quality products and services. Social skills training will ensure a smooth working relationship among core and assignment employees.

How to Make the Blended Workforce Work

The blended workforce has contributed to successful results for the companies that have employed it. We believe that there are two keys to success. The first is to develop a work culture and a teamwork environment to support the blended workforce. The second is to proactively deal with human resources issues in a timely manner to keep the program on track.

Develop the Culture and Teamwork

As we indicated in our portrait of the blended workforce, 50 percent of respondents report that core and assignment employees see each other as working harmoniously, and only 10 percent perceive that core and assignment employees are competing for the same jobs. Maintaining cooperation and reducing competition is a major factor affecting outcomes such as productivity and performance, and our respondents indicate significant productivity improvements. In order to build and maintain good working relationships, we recommend the proactive development of a compatible work culture among core and assignment employees. This is accomplished through the up-front definition of job fit characteristics to be used as selection criteria *for both workforces*. The selection process should produce side by side workforces sharing similar job-fit characteristics. The result should be job motivation and commitment to high performance.

Adopt a "blended" team approach to work design. Teams and teamwork are quickly becoming the norm in work venues across North America. A team approach to work supports flatter and leaner organizations, continuous improvement, and a multi-skilled workforce. The blended workforce presents a key issue of *balance* between separation and integration of people and work roles. Too much integration is not cost-effective and too little integration is disruptive. The key to an effective blended workforce is achieving a balanced approach through teamwork. Following are four recommendations for such an approach:

1. *Include temporary workers on teams.* Total integration of the assignment workforce onto teams enhances morale, commitment, and motivation. Integration includes, in general, attending team meetings and involvement in process improvement activities and important communications. However, the type of involvement will depend upon the types of teams that are utilized. Figure 7.12 provides a guide for including assignment employees on teams.

2. *Provide temporary workers with team training.* The team training for temporary assignment workers need not be as detailed or lengthy as the training for core workers. However, it should include basic team skills, team communication, and meeting behavior skills.

Figure 7.12 Involvement in Work Teams

Type of Team	Appropriate Involvement For Assignment Employees
Daily shift communication meetings	Attend all daily meetings
Cell manufacturing teams	Participate as member as long as in employment
Natural work teams comprising a process or function	Participate in team meetings as well as administrative functions of team
Project teams and task forces	Participate on team if appropriate for work role
Shop floor maintenance/ repair teams	Participate if maintenance task involves work of employee
Quality process improvement teams	Participate on team if appropriate for work role

3. *Communicate team role definition for assignment workers.* Due to the shorter tenure of assignment employees, their roles on teams will differ from that of core employees. For example, manufacturing assignment employees may be assigned to more repetitive tasks, while core employees may be required to participate in a wider set of work activities. The specific technical and social roles should be clearly defined by managers and team leaders and monitored over time.

4. *Provide team compensation for assignment employees that is parallel to that for core workers.* In many companies teams are compensated with bonuses or lump sum payments for reaching team milestones or for team performance. It is important that all team members receive some compensation, recognizing that the total compensation and benefits package for core and assignment employees will differ. It is straightforward to deliver bonuses (however they are determined) through the staffing

company employing the assignment employees. It need not be identical to the awards for the core employees, but it is important to provide team compensation for the *whole team.*

What We Have Learned: Steps Companies Should Take to Implement the Blended Workforce

For companies contemplating a blended workforce, we recommend the consideration of the following eight steps:

1. *Establish clear boundaries and skill requirements for the temporary/assignment workforce and the scope of involvement.* Make the blended workforce a strategic tool for competitive advantage by clearly defining the skills and tasks that will remain "core" and those that will be part of the temporary/assignment workforce. In addition, plan a specific component of the total workforce to be reserved for assignment employees on a seasonal as well as annual basis.

2. *Establish human resources policies and practices to support the blended workforce strategy.* Policies for staffing, training, career advancement, and general management should be aligned with the blended workforce strategy.

3. *Institute a selection and staffing program to ensure that the right skills are selected.* It is critical to have a seamless hiring process for both core and assignment employees. This will go a long way toward developing a strong work culture.

4. *Establish a combined communication program for the core and assignment workforce.* Another element for building a strong work culture is to have an integrated communication program that includes the assignment workforce in all major company meetings and media.

5. *Utilize an on-site manager for assignment (and contract) employees.* The manager will provide continuity to the assignment

workforce and a management framework essential for a smooth-running operation.

6. *Integrate assignment employees into teams.* Teamwork is not possible without specific roles and responsibilities outlined and communicated to all employees.

7. *Conduct job training for assignment employees.* Without proper training, assignment employees will not be able to contribute effectively. A long-term approach to training will involve a proper orientation as well as training for technical skills.

8. *Establish specific metrics to monitor productivity and quality performance.* These metrics include operational measurements such as unit cost as well as financial and customer-focused measures. It is important to clearly communicate the goals related to each measure and make sure that core as well as assignment employees understand the goals and how to reach them through their own work.

Note

1. "1996 Research Survey: Meeting Business Objectives with a Blended Workforce," William Olsten Center for Workforce Strategies, 1996. This survey was conducted jointly by the Olsten Center staff and the Center for Workforce Effectiveness.

8

The Economics of the Virtual Workplace

We've worked with a number of U.S.-based manufacturers in the process of establishing manufacturing operations in Latin America, where labor rates are typically much lower for similar kinds of work than in the U.S. One of the most frequent fallacies encountered among companies contemplating a move outside the U.S. is that low-cost labor is the key to economic success. In one case, several managers within a company required that labor rates go no higher than 73 pesos per day per worker (about $9.00 per day or $1.12 per hour given the then current U.S. exchange rate). Yet the company wanted to put the latest principles of lean manufacturing into place and had invested millions of dollars in state-of-the-art technology. The 73-peso-per-day mandate created serious limitations. For example:

- The level of skills they could recruit from the market
- The level of training they could invest to develop skills
- The degree to which workers could become versatile across key processes
- The company's ability to attract people and avoid high rates of employee turnover

We asked the managers, "What's so sacred about 73 pesos per day?" The answer was, "We need to reduce costs everywhere." We then asked the company's cost accountants to tell us what percentage of the total unit production cost would be represented by the labor costs in question. The answer was about 2 percent (this figure averages about 10 percent among U.S.-based manufacturers). We responded, "If you need to get cost out, you could fire everyone in sight and still have taken care of only 2 percent of your cost problem!"

Economic Realities of the Virtual Workplace

This example illustrates a major mistake that some U.S. companies are making today in the wholesale pursuit of cost cutting. Virtual work systems are *more* labor-intensive, not less labor-intensive. They cost *more*, not less. In fact, we find that labor cost per employee under a virtual work design averages 15 to 20 percent higher than under an equivalent traditional work design. The costs are threefold:

1. Higher wage costs
2. Higher training and development costs
3. Sufficient slack in the work schedule to allow people to move around and gain experience

Let's make one point extremely clear: Virtual workplaces are not for companies that need to cut labor cost; they are for companies that seek to enhance labor resources in order to leverage higher levels of business performance. The virtual workplace makes sense only when the company is looking for ways to combine people and technology in achieving high performance.

The higher labor cost per employee inherent in the virtual workplace forces us to make a business case for it. That is, we need to identify the offsetting benefits that justify the higher labor cost: higher productivity, lower product/service cost, shorter cycle times, and higher customer satisfaction. These benefits, inherent in the virtual workplace, create economic value that more than offsets the investments in labor.

Economic Value

The economic value created by the virtual workplace derives from such areas as the production floor, the sales force, the product development team, and the call center, to name just a few. The value flows from better operations as measured by operational metrics such as unit cost, uptime operating efficiency, fast cycle time, high quality, and minimum scrap.[1] The virtual workplace creates economic value at the margin by taking such metrics beyond the limits imposed by the traditional workplace. Anyone considering a transition to the virtual workplace must build a model to guide decision making. Such a model will facilitate how far and how fast one should move toward virtual workplace arrangements.

The Economic Model

The business case for the virtual workplace is based on a cost-benefit analysis that will allow us to decide if the financial return on the work design will justify the cost of developing and maintaining it. The model illustrated in Figure 8.1 shows the components of the business case for work design in a typical manufacturing environment. We have defined three levels of factors in the model:

1. *Economic value*—the economic value that accrues to the company for achieving its production and service commitments, high levels of customer loyalty and retention, dominant market share, and high levels of profitability.

2. *Drivers of economic value*—those factors that will be influenced by work design leading to or driving additional economic value. Such factors include productivity (labor and equipment), first pass quality (degree to which defects and rework are avoided), total unit cost (labor, material, overhead), inventory levels, and customer satisfaction.

3. *Virtual workplace factors*—those aspects of the workforce

Figure 8.1 Economic Model of a Work Design (Manufacturing Example)

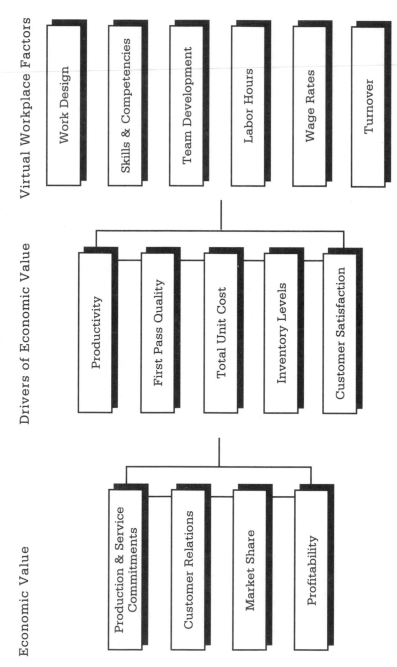

impacting the drivers. Such factors include work design, skills (degree of multiskilling and flexibility in the workforce), hours of labor, wage rates, and employee turnover.

The logic of the model is that economic value is derived from the factors that constitute the design of the virtual workplace through the drivers—those metrics of the business that define operations effectiveness. The model, therefore, allows us to assess the benefits to be derived that make the cost of a virtual workplace worth the investment. Using the model, we can tell how many additional dollars of economic value will accrue to the bottom line for each additional dollar of cost.

How to Put the Model to Use

Following is an overview of the six steps in putting the model to use.

Step 1. Establish Business Metrics and Set Goals for Economic Value

Identifying metrics requires understanding the business or business unit mission, its key measures, and the goals or objectives defining achievement on each measure. Key metrics and goals usually include the following:

- Achieving targeted levels of *production and service* (e.g., revenues)
- Achieving targeted levels of *customer satisfaction*
- Achieving targeted levels of *market share*
- Achieving targeted levels of *profitability*

Step 2. Identify Drivers of Economic Value

Once we've agreed upon how to measure economic value and set goals, we need to understand the mechanics of how to achieve them. Step 2 requires expert understanding of operations strategy and tactics. To define and set goals on metrics of productivity, cost, and quality, for example, we need to examine core business processes—procurement, transformation, and customer fulfillment—that will drive business results. Some experts characterize such drivers as *critical success factors (CSFs)*, things that must occur in order to achieve our economic value goals. Examples of such process drivers include:

- Achieving the highest levels of *first pass quality* in the industry
- Achieving reductions in *warranty claim* frequency and dollar amount
- Manufacturing products as efficiently as possible by using minimal *inventory* (the lowest level of materials and finished goods inventory possible)
- Achieving the highest levels of *productivity* in the industry
- Achieving the highest level of *customer service* in the industry
- Achieving the lowest levels of *total unit cost* in the industry

Step 3. Identify Virtual Workplace Factors That Will Unleash the Drivers

The third step is to identify workforce arrangements that we expect will influence the business drivers identified in step 2. Our research demonstrates that the following workforce factors will impact the drivers in the model:

- *Work design*—how we organize work, including work roles and career paths. In the virtual workplace, the work will be organized around core business processes, with minimal departmental and occupational barriers.

- *Skills and competencies*—greater breadth and depth of skills than in a traditional workplace. This means employees must be multiskilled and able to support an entire business process, yielding greater flexibility and labor productivity.

• *Team development*—making a team of employees responsible for an entire business process (e.g., establishing a new insurance policy). Organizing work into teams creates flexibility and productivity.

• *Labor hours*—a factor of production. The more hours spent in producing a unit, the more expensive that unit. The goal is to achieve high levels of output per hour of labor invested.

• *Wage rate*—the rate of pay (including base wage and benefits) that the company pays for each hour of labor. The higher the wage rate, the higher the cost of labor. Yet the wage rate must be sufficient for the company to attract and retain the highly skilled people required by the virtual workplace.

• *Turnover*—the replacement rate for workers. For example, in order to maintain an employment level of one hundred people this year, how many people do we have to hire? If we have to replace ten people to maintain the one hundred, our turnover rate is 10 percent. If we have to hire one hundred people to maintain the one hundred, our turnover rate is 100 percent. A certain amount of turnover is to be expected (for example, people retire, poor performers are let go), but too much can be very expensive. The costs of replacing an employee (e.g., recruitment, selection, lost productivity) can become quite expensive in the virtual workplace (from $10,000 to $15,000 per employee in some cases).

Step 4. Organize the Factors Into a Model

Steps 1 through 3 help us to understand the core economics of a business unit. The fourth step in building the business case requires that we organize the measures into a model that will allow us to measure cost versus benefit. We call such a model the Enterprise Report Card (ERC).

In building the ERC, we want to (1) define the measure, (2) understand its expected impact, and (3) define the economic impact of a unit improvement in the measure's performance. Figure 8.2 illustrates sample measures and their economic impact in a manufacturing plant. These measures include drivers of economic value and workplace factors.

Next, we review each measure independently and identify its related economic impact. In addition, we want to set a goal for improvement that can be attributed to virtual workplace arrangements. Such an analysis requires an intimate look at the business, as each business will have unique measures and relationships. Following is the analysis for a vehicle manufacturing plant:

Figure 8.2 Sample Measurements for an Enterprise Report Card

Measure Type	Measure	Definition	Expected Impact
Driver of value	First time quality	Percentage of units with no defects to be repaired	Each unit that is defect-free reduces the cost of rework and repair, contributing directly to reduction in total unit cost
Driver of value	Warranty claims	Frequency and amount involved in resolving warranty claims	Each dollar reduction in warranty cost reduces total unit cost
Driver of value	Number of day's supply inventory	Day's inventory carried to produce a given number of units	Each day's reduction of inventory necessary directly reduces total unit cost

(*continues*)

Figure 8.2 (*continued*)

Measure Type	Measure	Definition	Expected Impact
Driver of value	Productivity	Total labor hours/unit	Each reduction in hours per unit directly reduces total unit cost
Workplace factor	Head count	Number of people employed during a year	The lower the level of head count for a given year's production, the lower total unit cost
Workplace factor	Wage cost	The hourly compensation (wage per hour) paid to employees	The higher the wage rate, the higher the labor cost (wage rate X labor hours). Labor cost contributes directly to total unit cost
Workplace factor	Training cost	The additional cost (including time and materials) for training skills	Training cost contributes directly to total unit cost

1. First Time Quality (FTQ)

Average labor cost per repair incident:	$100
Average material cost per repair incident:	$500
Units produced per year:	15,000

Baseline FTQ:	88%
FTQ goal—virtual workplace:	96%
Improvement due to workforce effectiveness:	8% (88–96%)

Economic Impact Calculation:

$$8\% \times 15{,}000 \text{ units} = 1{,}200 \text{ additional units defect-free}$$

$$1{,}200 \times (\$100 + \$500) = \$720{,}000 \text{ cost savings from FTQ improvement}$$

2. Warranty Claims

Average warranty unit cost:	$5,000
Units produced per year:	15,000
Baseline warranty claim (per 1,000):	329
Warranty claim goal (per 1,000):	200
Improvement due to workforce effectiveness (per 1,000):	129 (329 – 200) fewer complaints/1,000 units produced

Economic Impact Calculation:

$$(129 \div 1{,}000) \times 15{,}000 \text{ units} = 1{,}935 \text{ fewer claims}$$

$$1{,}935 \times \$500 = \$967{,}500 \text{ cost savings due to fewer claims}$$

3. Day's Supply Inventory

Material cost per unit:	$20,000
Units produced per day:	42
Cost of financing inventory:	5%
Baseline day's inventory:	10
Day's inventory goal—virtual workplace:	6

Improvement due to workforce   4 days (10 – 6)
effectiveness:

Economic Impact Calculation:

42 units X $20,000
material cost per day = $840,000

5% finance cost X
$840,000 material
    cost per day = $42,000 annual savings by
reducing day's inventory by
one day

4 days X $42,000 = $168,000 cost savings over
one year due to improved
inventory efficiency

4. Productivity (Hours per Unit)

Wage rate:	$15.00/hour
Units produced per year:	15,000
Number of employees:	250
Average hours worked per employee:	2,080
Number of labor hours per year:	250 employees X 2,080 hours = 520,000
Baseline hours per unit:	520,000 hours/year ÷ 15,000 units = 34.7
Hours per unit goal—virtual workplace:	27.7
Improvement due to workforce effectiveness:	7 (34.7 – 27.7)

Economic Impact Calculation:

(7 hours X $15.00)
       X 15,000 = $1,575,000 cost savings due
to improved productivity

5. Head Count

Load on annual compensation	
(benefits, insurance):	$12,550
Baseline head count:	250
*Virtual workplace goal**	200
Improvement in head count:	= 50 (250 − 200)

Economic Impact Calculation:

50 fewer heads X $12,550 = $627,500 cost savings due
to improved head count

6. Wage Cost

Baseline hourly wage rate:	$15
Wage rate—virtual workplace:	$18
Recommended head count—virtual workplace:	200
Planned annual hours per person:	2,080
Wage cost growth (average hours per person):	$3 ($18 − $15)

*a. Hours per unit (see 4):	27.7
b. Units produced per year:	15,000
c. Revised hours:	415,500 (27.7 X 15,000)
d. Average hours per employee (see 4):	2,080
e. New required head counts:	200 (415,500 ÷ 2,080)

Economic Impact Calculation:

$3.00 X (200 X 2,080
hours) = $1,248,000 additional cost
due to higher wage rates

7. Training Cost

Baseline training hours per employee:	24
Recommended training hours—virtual workplace:	60

> *Additional training hours per employee:*   36 (60 – 24)
> *Recommended head count:*   200
> *Training cost per hour:* $30

Economic Impact Calculation:

($30 training cost per
hour X 36 additional
hours X 200 people) = $216,000 additional cost
due to increased training

The work in step 4 can be summarized in a completed ERC that sets goals and expresses the economic value created by achieving them in the virtual workplace. See Figure 8.3 for an ERC that demonstrates how workplace factors and the drivers of value contribute to the economics of the business.

One of our clients characterizes the drivers of economic value in Figure 8.3 as "dials on the dashboard." He notes that these are the critical measures he concentrates on when running his business. "If I make the numbers on the dashboard, I know the ultimate measures of economic value will follow. If I don't make the numbers, they won't." He also recognizes that he must take care of virtual workforce factors in order to "make the numbers on the dashboard." In this case the ERC shows that the investment of an additional $1,464,000 in work design, training, and compensation in the first year will yield an additional $2,217,500 in economic value for a return rate in the first year of 1.51 to 1.

The analysis thus far shows that there are tradeoffs associated with instituting a virtual workplace. The virtual workplace represents an investment, just like any other in business. The first five items in the analysis in step 4 are sources of economic benefit: first-time quality improvement, warranty claim reduction, inventory reduction, productivity (hours per unit) improvement, and lower head count. Items 6 and 7 represent the additional costs associated with a virtual workplace (higher wages and higher training costs). The ERC shows the net benefit (benefit less cost) to be expected from a virtual workplace in the

Figure 8.3 Example Economic Cost-Benefit Model

	Measure	Baseline	Goal	Impact
Benefit	FTQ	88%	96%	$ 720,000
	Warranty claims	329 per 1,000	200 per 1,000	967,500
	Day's supply inventory level	10 days	6 days	168,000
	Productivity	34.7 hrs./unit	27.7 hrs./unit	1,575,000
	Head count	250	200	627,500
Total benefits				$4,058,000
Costs associated with benefits	Wages		+20%	$1,248,000
	Training		+36 hours per person per year	216,000
Total costs				$1,464,000
Net benefit				$2,594,000
Return ratio				1.77:1

first year of operation. The analysis can then be expanded over an entire planning horizon (e.g., three to five years).

Step 5. Perform Sensitivity Analysis and Validate

Before a decision is made, we need to satisfy two concerns:

1. Where are the major sources of influence on economic results? Where can we get the biggest impact through workforce arrangements?
2. How do we know that a virtual workplace (investing in skills, training, and work design) will actually result in the impact promised by the model?

We address the first question by conducting "what if" analyses called *sensitivity analyses.* In this process, the model is used to quantify the economic impact of unit changes in drivers and work design features. If we are contemplating a higher wage rate, for example, the impact on cash flow can easily be tested by varying that parameter. Sensitivity analysis allows us to accomplish two outcomes: (1) We can quickly test the impact the alternative policies; (2) we can see the relative impact of various drivers and policies on the model's results. We might find, for example, that wage rate variation has much less impact on total unit cost than first pass quality or inventory costs.

The second question is a far more difficult one, but it must be addressed just the same. By nature, the economic model is an abstraction from reality, a simplification. The user of the model has the right to ask, "How do I know this thing really works?" or, "How can you prove that it's the work design—not the equipment—that delivers performance improvement?"

Several issues must be considered in order to satisfactorily resolve such challenges to the model. First, in the real world, simple cause-and-effect relationships rarely exist. For example, the workforce factors by themselves don't have an impact on performance, just as the technology by itself has no impact. Performance improvement is created by the combination of workforce factors and technology. In strict scientific jargon, the workforce factors identified in our model are *necessary but not sufficient* conditions for performance improvement. Perhaps the old marketing adage applies: If you are unsure if you are getting your money's worth from advertisers, try *not* advertising some day.

Second, relationships modeled in the ERC (e.g., the impact of multiskilling on productivity) must be based on expert knowledge of the system itself—as it operates in the real world. Thus, the judgment that multiskilling yields a 20 percent improvement in productivity over traditional work designs must be based on four sources of evidence:

1. *Expert logic behind the model.* Workforce experts are familiar with work design. Their logic, on its face, should provide compelling reason to expect the impact predicted by the model.

2. *Empirical evidence.* The facts must also be brought to bear. Previous experience and actual results in similar situations are our most important sources of evidence. Benchmarking provides a critical source of information, allowing us to confirm and rely on the model.

3. *Experience of others.* Although somewhat less systematic than empirical evidence, the experience of other companies will be extremely compelling in making decisions. We have yet to encounter the executive who hasn't asked us, "How did this work in other companies in our industry? What did they find?"

4. *Our own experience.* Ultimately, the most convincing evidence of a model's validity is the organization's own experience. That's why we strongly recommend that our customers making workforce changes use their own model to constantly track actual achievement against goals. Such tracking ensures that the workforce changes will continue to have impact and provide the basis for constantly renewing and improving operational effectiveness as the business grows and evolves.

The key to success with economic models is to pretest, test, validate, and constantly revise on the basis of actual results.

Step 6. Establish the Cost-Benefit and Decide

The last step in economic modeling is to establish the cost-benefit of the virtual workplace and decide whether or not to proceed. If the decision is yes, then we must be prepared to employ the model continuously for as long as we have the work system in place to periodically evaluate and ensure that the predicted results are, in fact, being achieved.

Business Case: Food Products Manufacturer

A large processor and distributor of frozen seafood products followed the business case method for analyzing the impact that the transition to virtual workplace arrangements (including work redesign and skill-based pay) would have on its profitability.

Step 1. Establish Business (Plant) Metrics and Set Goals for Economic Value

The plant leadership identified three key metrics of the business:

1. *Materials cost.* Raw material drives costs in the seafood business. "Shrimp are jewels," commented one manager. Raw material is the largest component of the total cost (about 40 percent) for the manufacturer. New work designs were expected to vastly improve the company's management of raw materials including scrap and process loss.

2. *Labor productivity.* Labor is a key driver of cost management and profitability. Improved labor productivity is a key objective of the new work design. Although the labor cost (wages, training) per employee may rise, the company can take on increased production without having to add to its head count, because individual labor productivity has increased.

3. *Overhead.* Overhead costs include the salaries of indirect employees and the costs of utilities, maintenance, and all other costs of production other than direct labor and materials. The plant's goal is to increase the efficiency of overhead, i.e., maximize the output-per-unit overhead cost.

Step 2. Identify Drivers of Economic Value

The plant then identified the most important drivers of value:

- *Process loss.* Waste must be reduced as much as possible.
- *Productivity.* Labor must be made as productive as possible. Production per labor hour will be increased under the new work design by reducing the number of temporary employee hours worked and decreasing the number of production days necessary to produce a year's worth of product. Work design and cross-training will impact labor productivity.
- *Overhead.* Several overhead drivers are important under the shift to virtual arrangements. A better-trained and better-motivated workforce could be expected to incur fewer safety incidents or accidents. Cross-training will afford a lower head count in the quality, maintenance, and sanitation areas of the facility as well.

Step 3. Identify Virtual Workplace Factors That Will Unleash the Drivers

Next, the plant's management analyzed workforce factors that would drive economic value:

- *Wage cost.* The implementation of skill-based pay was expected to drive up the total wage cost for the facility, particularly during the first three to four years of the program. The costs would be incurred because employees would be increasing their skills and thus compensated more for them under a skill-based pay program.

• *Training cost.* Training of the workforce was expected to increase dramatically. Components included in estimating training were the cost of program development, cost of training materials such as guidebooks produced for the entire workforce, and cost of delivery incurred by professional trainers.

• *Turnover cost.* Turnover was expected to increase during the first few years under the new work system and then decrease afterwards. The early increase would occur because those who did not wish to cross-train would find the new environment uncomfortable and leave. Afterward, turnover was expected to drop because those who stayed would be more satisfied with their work and pay.

Step 4. Organize the Factors Into a Model

Once the key drivers and workplace factors of the model were identified, the next step was to develop an Enterprise Report Card that allowed us to assess cost versus benefit or the return on investment in the virtual workplace. Each measure identified by the plant management and the measure's expected impact is outlined in Figure 8.4.

Each measure was then analyzed independently to assess impact. See the calculation of each impact as calculated for year 1 beginning below and continuing on page 230.

1. Process loss

Unit cost of materials:	$0.10/pound
Daily material input:	100,000 pounds/day
Working days:	360 days/year
Current process loss (annually):	5%
Estimated improvement (annual improvement):	1.25 percentage points annually

Economic Impact Calculation (Year 1):

Figure 8.4 Enterprise Report Card Measures and Expected Impact for a Food Processor

Measure Type	Measure	Definition	Expected Impact
Driver of value	Process loss	(Input material–output material)/ input material	Increasing the amount of output for the same amount of input significantly affects the total cost of the facility
Driver of value	Temporary employee hours worked	Change in total hours worked by temporary employees	Since total of input materials is held constant, the analysis will look at improvement in pounds handled per hour. This improvement will be applied to the reduction in temporary employee hours.
Driver of value	Number of production days	Change in number of days of production	Fewer production days result in overall savings to the facility

(continues)

Figure 8.4 (*continued*)

Measure Type	Measure	Definition	Expected Impact
Driver of value	Safety incidents	Each safety incident costing on average several thousand dollars to resolve	Fewer incidents increase profitability of the facility
Workplace factor	Head count	Impact of each employee's compensation and benefits on total cost	Fewer employees compensation and benefits
Workplace factor	Wage cost	The hourly compensation paid to participants in the work design	Wage rates will increase due to employees gaining skills and achieving higher pay levels
Workplace factor	Training cost	Total cost of development and delivery of training	Training has to be developed. Each employee will then receive a higher level of training than in a conventional work design

(*continues*)

Figure 8.4 (*continued*)

Measure Type	Measure	Definition	Expected Impact
Workplace factor	Turnover cost	Cost of replacing one employee	Each employee who leaves incurs a cost to the facility to replace and train. The facility also loses productivity during the new hire's ramp-up

100,000 lbs. daily input
X 0.0125 change = 1,250 lbs. saved daily

1,250 lbs saved daily
X $0.10 cost per lb. = $125 saved daily

$125 saved daily X
360 working days = $45,000 saved

2. Hours Worked by Temporary Employees

Number of temporary employees:	234
Average hours per temporary employee per year (current):	500
Average hours per temporary employee per year (year 1):	400
Average hours per temporary employee per year (year 5):	40
Hourly wage rate (cost to company):	$11.25
Expected reduction in temporary hours (year 1):	100
Expected reduction in temporary hours (year 5):	480

Economic Impact Calculation (Year 1):

500 hours – 400 hours = 100 hours less per temporary employee

100 hours per temporary employee X 234 temporary employees = 23,400 hours

23,400 hours less X $11.25 per hour = $263,250 saved (fewer temporary employee hours required)

3. Production Days

Straight-time production day cost*:	$5,500
Fewer production days (annually over baseline) (year 1):	2
Fewer production days (annually over baseline) (year 5):	10

Economic Impact Calculation (Year 1):

2 fewer production days X $5,500 straight-time production cost = $11,000 saved

4. Safety Incidents

Cost to resolve a safety incident:	$5,000
Baseline number of incidents:	15/year
Expected reduction in safety incidents (year 1):	7%
Expected reduction in safety incidents (year 5):	20%

---

*Accounting process expert's estimate based on knowledge of the business and cost structure.

Economic Impact Calculation (Year 1):

15 incidents X 7%
fewer incidents in
year 1 = 1 less incident

1 less incident X $5,000
cost per incident = $5,000 saved

5. Head Count

Fully loaded annual compensation
($7.50/hour base pay plus benefits,
insurance, etc.): $22,000
Fewer support staff required
(year 1):   3
Fewer support staff required (year 5):   6

Economic Impact Calculation (Year 1):

3 fewer employees X
22,000 per year = $66,000 saved

6. Wage Cost

Current average wage (baseline) (year 1): $7.15/hour
Current average wage (baseline) (year 5): $8.36/hour
Skill-based average wage (year 1): $7.50
Skill-based average wage (year 5): $10.00
Number of employees: 50

Economic Impact Calculation (Year 1):

$7.50 – $7.15 = $0.35 increase

$0.35 increase X
2,080 hours per
person per year = $728/person on average

$728 per person X
50 employees = $36,400 additional total
wage cost

7. Turnover

Estimated cost of replacing an *employee:*	$1,100
Additional turnover declines (year 1):	4.5% higher
Additional turnover declines (year 5):	20% lower

Economic Impact Calculation (Year 1):

4% increase X
50 employees = 2 more
employees leave

2 more leave X
$1,000 cost to replace = $2,000 additional cost

8. Training Cost

Cost to develop materials/program:	$10,000 (one-time cost)
Cost of materials (year 1):	$10,000
Cost of materials (year 5):	$12,155
Cost of delivery (additional training time per trainer) (year 1):	$36,000
(Training is gradually brought in-house) (year 5):	$9,000

Economic Impact Calculation (Year 1):

$10,000 development
cost + $10,000 material
cost + $36,000
delivery cost = $56,000 additional cost

After the eight measures were identified and analyzed, the data could be organized into an Enterprise Report Card. The ERC defined each measure and showed the baseline value for the measure in a traditional work setting, the change expected in the virtual workplace, and the additional economic value created. Figure 8.5 illustrates such a report card.

Next, the cost and benefit factors were organized into a five-year impact analysis, as shown in Figure 8.6.

The payback from moving to a virtual workplace in this case was $1,957,661 or a benefit-cost ratio of more than 4.55 during the first five years following the change. That means that for every additional dollar spent beyond what would have been spent in a traditional workplace, the company stood to benefit an additional $4.55.

Step 5. Perform Sensitivity Analysis and Validate

The management team ran several scenarios in order to ensure that the workplace arrangements would be successful at the facility. Several conditions were manipulated to test how each measure would affect the plant's performance. One such test was to establish the break-even to determine the minimum performance required to obtain a positive net impact.

Step 6. Establish the Cost-Benefit and Decide

When it was determined that a positive net impact could be achieved, the company decided to proceed with implementation. Using the targeted levels of performance improvements as a gauge for success, subsequent follow-up analyses have confirmed the payback.

The Discipline of a Business Case

The economic modeling in this chapter was driven by a conviction that financial investment in human resources in the virtual

Figure 8.5 Completed ERC (Year 1)

	Measure	Baseline	Goal	Impact
Benefit	Process loss	5.00%	3.75%	$ 45,000
	Temporary employee hours worked	500 hours/ person	400 hours/ person	263,250
	Production days	360 production days	358 production days	11,000
	Safety incidents	15 incidents	14 incidents	5,000
	Head count	50 support staff	47 support staff	66,000
Total benefits				$390,250
Costs associated with benefits	Wage cost		+5% year	$ 36,400
	Turnover cost		+4 percentage points year 1	2,000
	Training cost		Additional cost of development, materials, and delivery	56,000
Total costs				$ 94,400
Net benefit				$295,850
Return ratio				3.13:1

Figure 8.6 Five-Year Economic Impact Analysis for a Food Processor

Benefits	Year 1	Year 2	Year 3	Year 4	Year 5	Total
Process loss	$ 45,000	$ 57,308	$ 76,410	$ 95,513	$ 114,615	$ 388,846
Hours worked	263,250	263,655	265,587	266,979	267,872	1,327,343
Production days	11,000	24,750	33,000	46,750	55,000	170,500
Safety incidents	5,000	10,000	15,000	15,000	15,000	60,000
Head count	66,000	71,516	89,991	101,145	112,299	440,951
Subtotal	$390,250	$427,229	$479,988	$525,387	$564,787	$2,387,640
Costs						
Wage cost	$ 36,400	$ 45,656	$ 53,722	$ 60,551	$ 66,093	$ 262,423
Turnover	2,000	$ 175	($ 1,900)	($ 4,225)	($ 6,250)	($ 10,200)
Training cost	56,000	46,500	29,025	25,076	21,155	177,756
Subtotal	94,400	92,331	80,847	81,402	80,998	429,979
Net total	$ 295,850	$334,897	$399,141	$443,985	$483,789	$1,957,661
Return ratio	3.13	4.63	5.94	6.45	6.97	4.55

workplace had to be held to the same cost-benefit discipline that any investment was held. We have demonstrated a tool that can be used to estimate the costs and benefits of work redesign, pay systems, and training inherent in the virtual workplace. Using the model effectively requires a shift of thinking away from labor as purely a cost. In the virtual workplace, people are an asset and financial investment is seen as an investment in future performance.

Note

1. Note that our use of the term *economic value* is much narrower and closer to operations than the often cited metric of Economic Value Added (EVA). See Joel M. Stern, G. Bennett Stewart, and Donald Chew, *Corporate Restructuring and Executive Compensation* (Cambridge Mass.: Ballinger Publishing, 1989).

9

Getting to the New Deal in the Virtual Workplace

In Chapter 1 we stated that the virtual workplace requires a New Deal for employment. We claimed that establishing a New Deal to replace the Old Deal that has been shattered is the single most important challenge to our economy in the next decade. Finally, we noted that although we have not completely filled the void, many forward-thinking companies are taking actions that will, indeed, create a New Deal for employment in the twenty-first century. In subsequent chapters, we outlined a virtual work design, a new set of skills, work organized around business processes, rewards oriented away from a "job" and toward economic value creation, and employment defined according to a blended workforce. One final question remains: How do we get there?

We have had the opportunity to work with many companies creating the New Deal, and can learn from their experience. Following is a road map consisting of the steps winners have taken to finally achieve the work and reward arrangements that will prove successful in the next decades.

Step 1: Get Past Future Shock

Change is scary and painful. Alvin Toffler has characterized the anxieties arising from the changes he described in *Future*

Shock and *Power Shift*.[1] Almost every time a company moves to virtual arrangements, the prospect creates future shock. It is stressful for employees and managers, young and old. In fact, the reactions of many people caught up in the organizational upheavals of the 1990s fit a pattern identified over thirty years ago by Dr. Elisabeth Kübler-Ross among people who have been diagnosed with a fatal disease.[2] The stages (and associated organizational anxieties) are illustrated in Figure 9.1. Both organizations and individual employees must get past these stages in order to take positive steps in creating a New Deal.

Getting to a New Deal means getting past denial, anger, bargaining, and depression to acceptance that the Old Deal is gone—and is not coming back. The reality is that globalization of business and the technological revolution have made going back impossible. Acceptance gets us past recrimination, hand-wringing, and sadness to a positive state that allows us to shift para-

Figure 9.1 Getting Past Future Shock

Stage	Organization Anxiety	Employee Anxiety
Denial	"This is a blip. We'll tough it out and business will be back."	"They can't really mean it! These things don't happen here!"
Anger	"Why can't they leave us alone! They don't play fair!"	"How dare they do this to loyal employees!"
Bargaining	"If we get lucky, a little tweaking will do. We promise—this is the last layoff!"	"Maybe if I work harder!"
Depression	"What's the use?"	"It's hopeless!"
Acceptance	The New Deal	The New Deal

digms and look for creative arrangements that will allow us to thrive. Getting past future shock, then, is the first step.

Step 2: Think Processes, Not Jobs

Globalization and the technological revolution force us to focus on processes—the core processes that define our businesses and the support processes necessary for them to thrive. Truly thinking according to processes forces a painful shift in work paradigms from the job (where everything was neatly bundled) to the process (customer fulfillment), as illustrated in Figure 9.2. In our example, the way we look at work activities must move away from functions, departments, and jobs (sales, marketing, manufacturing, and distribution) to a single, fluid process (customer fulfillment).

The shift requires us to stop thinking about functions (with handoffs from sales to manufacturing to distribution) and start thinking about a seamless process that begins and ends with customers. The shift also requires us to stop thinking about jobs when organizing work and to start thinking about broad roles and career paths on teams, as illustrated in Figure 9.3. In this shift employees must go from thinking of their work in individual jobs with accountability for individual results to thinking of their broad role on a team.

In the future, employees will be part of a team. The shift will require individuals to take on a greater breadth and depth of accountability. Work will require more skills. It will consist of a greater variety of activities and will take individuals across traditional functional and job boundaries. Employees will see more of the process—they will interact with customers. Working in a process rather than a job will require them to raise their sights from individual job performance to process metrics related to the entire business. Thus, individual productivity will be subordinate to overall process productivity. Members of teams will be held jointly accountable for entire system results. The phrases "It's not my job" and "It would have worked if the other guy had done his job" will be unacceptable in the future.

Figure 9.2 The Move From Jobs to Processes

From:
Function/Department/Job

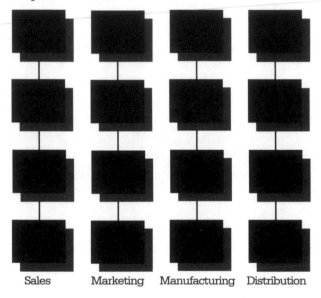

Sales   Marketing   Manufacturing   Distribution

To:
Process (Customer Fulfillment)

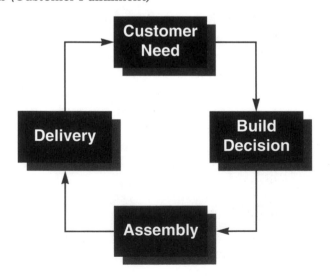

Figure 9.3 The Move From Jobs to Team Roles

From:
Narrow Jobs

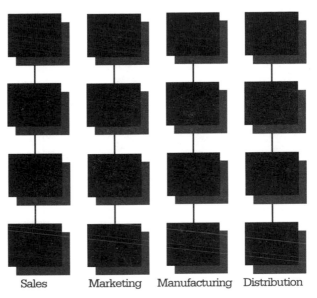

Sales   Marketing   Manufacturing   Distribution

To:
Broad Roles on Teams

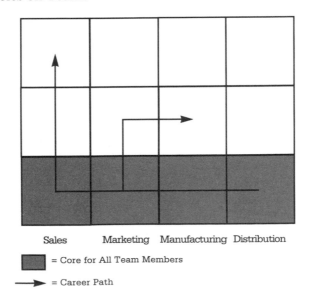

Sales   Marketing   Manufacturing   Distribution

■ = Core for All Team Members

➜ = Career Path

Step 3: Develop Virtual Relationships

Just as the New Deal tethers individual employees in teams, so will it require greater intimacy among players in value chains (vendors, suppliers, manufacturers, customers). Virtual relationships among suppliers and customers (the Borg-Warner–Ford relationship discussed in Chapter 4), among joint ventures (Sony and Corning forming American Video Glass to produce cathode ray tube glass), and among managers and unions have become the rule. The reason for virtual relationships is to take speed, efficiency, quality, cost-effectiveness, and customer satisfaction where it has never been before. Accomplishing such performance requires the intimacy of the cyberlink model described in Chapter 3.

Step 4: Evaluate Economic Impact

All choices in the virtual workplace must be examined under the discipline of cost/benefit modeling, described in Chapter 8. Organizations and individuals who do not add value in the virtual workplace will not be there long—that is a cold reality. In allocating scarce resources, then, organizations must ask, "What is our business?" and then, "What competencies do we need to deploy in order to outdistance our competitors?" Asking these questions necessarily involves considering foundation, core support, and outsourced competencies (see Figure 9.4).

For example, the football coach thinks first of filling key roles on the team; filling jobs for taking tickets is secondary. The coach will begin with foundation competencies, those capabilities we expect all players to bring to the organization. Each player must serve up these foundation competencies on his own. The coach will next turn to core competencies. Core competencies are central to the core process of the organization, and that is where we generate economic impact. Core competencies are where we need to marshal resources such as work design, rewards, staffing, training, and development. Support competencies are secondary in importance to the core. Getting to the New

Figure 9.4 Evaluation of Economic Impact

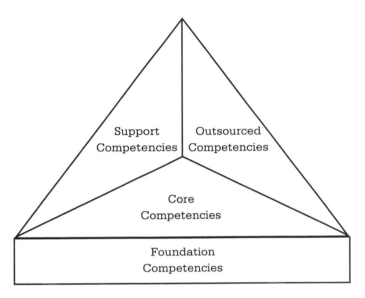

Deal, then, will require organizations to demand that employees bring basic foundation competencies such as math, writing, communication, and interpersonal qualities to the table as part of the deal. These "tickets into the ballpark" will be acquired by employees on their own time. U.S. companies are finding that the cost of remedial training for new labor market entrants without foundation skills is just too high. It has placed them at a competitive disadvantage compared to Asian and Western European companies whose labor forces gain such skills through primary and secondary education.

The coach in our example must eventually get to the process of ticket sales. Increasingly under the New Deal, companies find that the support processes, although necessary, are not central to the organization's strategy. Thus, they will consider outsourcing these processes to vendors who can do them better. Increasingly, in the virtual workplace, we will see outsourcing through the establishment of the virtual relationships described under step 3.

Step 5: Blend Your Workforce

Steps 3 and 4 call for organizations to establish virtual relationships and focus workforce arrangements on core competencies. Accomplishing these steps will result in a blended workforce—a heterogeneous mix of core employees, temporary employees, and contract employees, as well as of employees of suppliers and customers in the same workplace—and even on the same team!

Getting to the New Deal will require a shift away from the paradigm that all employees in the workplace are full-time, permanent employees. Blended teams will become the rule, not the exception. Skill paths and work designs will need to accommodate temporary and contract employees. Group incentives will need to embrace all members of the team, not just core, full-time, permanent employees. Training and development decisions must focus on achieving the right blend of full-time and temporary employees on a team. Designers of human resources policies will have to treat a blended workforce as an ongoing reality of business, not as a temporary arrangement.

Step 6: Manage Careers

The most sacred icon of the Old Deal was the *career*. If an employee had a career, it meant that he or she was guaranteed lifetime security in exchange for loyalty. It meant having a job (usually with a series of hierarchical promotions) until retirement with the same company. It meant receiving lifetime retirement benefits after retirement. The deal included defined-benefit pensions (often paying a substantial portion of one's top five years' earnings) and retirement health coverage.

Under the Old Deal, then, a career was a sinecure or a property right. Part of the anger at the passing of the Old Deal comes from the property owner whose property has been taken away. Obviously, the New Deal cannot guarantee lifetime employment, lifetime income, and health security, but can it offer something in the way of careers?

Yes. We believe careers will exist in the New Deal, and that they will be fulfilling. But responsibility for the career will shift from being solely an accountability of the company to becoming a joint accountability of the employer and the employee. We predict that the career paradigm will shift as follows: A new labor market entrant will view a career as a sequence of jobs held until retirement. The career, then, will not be defined by the job I hold (remember, the "job" has died). The career, instead, will be seen as an individual platform or asset. The platform will consist of the individual skills and competencies I hold at any point in time. How successful my career is will depend on *how closely aligned my skills are to the core business needs of the employer.* If we were advising a graduating student about getting ahead in the New Deal, we would counsel as follows: "Think of your current or prospective employer as your best customer. Ask yourself, 'What does my customer need most?' Make sure that the skill you have—your capacity to work—is and stays central to your customer's basic needs." Twenty years ago, high-tech companies needed the skills of electrical engineers because there were major challenges involved with electronic equipment. Today, those same companies need software engineers, because their major challenges involve application of software, rather than hardware. The lesson seems clear. The successful career in engineering is one that has shifted the skills platform over time. The job has not changed, but the skills required have. The engineer who is going to get ahead is the one who sees the change coming, anticipates the skills that will be needed, and gets them!

Careers in the New Deal will not consist of a sequence of promotions within the same company based on traditional performance decisions. Careers in the New Deal will consist of a platform upon which skills central to the changing needs of the company will be built, renewed, and expanded. Career movement and career pay, therefore, will be driven by increasing personal asset value—not loyalty.

Who should be responsible for managing this platform? Our answer: the employee. He or she will hold primary responsibility, and the company will hold secondary responsibility. The

New Deal will require us to act as adults, not children. Adults look out for themselves; they anticipate change and take action. Children expect (correctly) to be taken care of by parents and families. Getting to the New Deal, therefore, will require a major shift in thinking and behavior on the part of employees. It will require them to take primary responsibility for managing their careers. A career may well take an employee across several different companies, several different occupations, and several different countries. A career under the New Deal will require employees to assess their employers, asking themselves, "Is my company going in the right direction? Should I be looking elsewhere?" Thus, employees should assess employers just as employers now assess employees.

Over the years, we have worked with several companies that were in trouble. There was a pattern to their problems: Market share had dwindled; competitors had acquired the market and were taking operations global, producing at far lower cost and far higher profit; products were of inferior quality. While it did not take an expert to see this pattern, each of these companies' employees were unaware of these problems, let alone concerned. Problems like quality, cost, and product viability were the responsibility of management. When the day of reckoning came, who would be responsible for the failure? Managements? The employees? The unions? Under the New Deal, the question will be irrelevant. Under the New Deal, we will expect employees to have anticipated the environment as we now expect management to do. Under the New Deal, we will not predict that employees will go down with the ship. Under the New Deal, the best employees will gravitate towards the best companies.

The New Deal is not a simple matter of economic Darwinism, however. We foresee in the New Deal that companies will anticipate change and provide the opportunities (through work assignments and training) for employees to renew and add to their platforms. But employees will have to take advantage of assignment opportunities and training when they arise. They cannot sit back and expect to be taken care of.

Step 7: Practice Tough Love

The New Deal will require mutual accountability on the part of employers and employees. Getting to that accountability will require what people in the Appalachian cultures of West Virginia, eastern Kentucky, and eastern Tennessee call *tough love.* Tough love is the quality of confronting difficulties without sugar-coating them or denying that they exist. Tough love means taking short-term steps that may be painful but are necessary to succeed.

The Old Deal's parent-to-child relationship worked well as long as the manager, as parent, could single-handedly protect the family from the environment. But events have taken that protection away. Management can no longer guarantee lifetime employment. Managers can no longer deal with skill obsolescence by finding something for older employees to do even if the cost cannot be justified.

Tough love calls for the model to shift from a parent-child relationship to a partnership. Quite simply, employers and employees should be seen as partners. Under that vision, the relationship between the two shifts:

From	*To*
Parent/child	Mutual responsibility
Parent/child	Shared risk
Parent/child	Shared accountability

Getting to the New Deal requires the efforts and commitment of companies, employees, and unions. It will not happen unless all parties set clear business goals with stretch objectives, clearly define and act on the change in culture that will be necessary, clearly define and embrace new work roles on teams that go far beyond current job definitions, embrace customers as the ultimate definition of business success, and embrace continuous change and improvement in workplace technology.

Choosing this road and following this map will, indeed, determine whether we will achieve the New Deal.

Notes

1. Alvin Toffler, *Future Shock.* New York: Bantam Books, 1990; and Alvin Toffler, *Powershift.* New York: Bantam Books, 1990.
2. Elisabeth Kübler-Ross, *On Death And Dying.* New York: Collier Books, 1993.

Index

251